The *Savvy* Money Gal

6 Savvy Money Strategies *for* SUCCESSFUL WOMEN

Dear Kathleen & Archie,

Thank you for all
of your support.
Happy Reading!

Anita
XO KT

Dear Kathleen + Arlie,

Thank you guys and
of your support.

Happy Reading!

Trista
xo

The *Savvy* Money Gal

6 Savvy Money Strategies *for* SUCCESSFUL WOMEN

Anita Saulite

First Published in Canada 2013 by Influence Publishing

Cover Design: Marla Thompson
Typesetting: Greg Salisbury
Author Photographer: Christopher Gentile

To my family Patrick, Kyle, Chloe, and Skyler
for the love and patience you have given me
in becoming the woman I am today.

Testimonials

"Money matters do not have to be unmanageable, intimidating, or headache inducing. In her book, Anita uses her expertise to help readers break their bad money habits, and gain clarity and confidence when it comes to making the right money choices."
Pattie Lovett-Reid, CTV Chief Financial Commentator

"Many families feel the strain of bad financial habits. Anita presents unique insight on the link between financial well-being, and the well-being of our relationships with family, friends, and our own selves. Her book sheds light on a clear path for people to come out of their financial rut to embrace a new consciousness when it comes to their finances."
Scarlet Paolicchi, Founder of Family Focus Blog

"Our relationship with money is one of the strongest life metaphors that reflects our frozen beliefs about ourselves and our capacities. When we pursue a focused examination of these automatic habits and begin to challenge and change the entrenched beliefs and patterns that grip us, we can open to more personal freedom. In this book, Anita aims to de-clutter our mind of negative attitudes we have towards money, to become more mindful of money decisions, and to use money effectively to achieve personal goals. Through Anita's advice on healthy financial decision-making, she illuminates the bigger picture of attaining both financial and personal empowerment."
Catherine Comuzzi Ed.D. Cg Psychology, Psychotherapist and Master Coach Trainer

"When women have control over their finances, there is a powerful ripple effect: it provides more opportunity and stability for their children, it creates stronger communities, and it leads to a more prosperous society for all. Anita kick-starts the process with a step-by-step guide to help women take the reins of their own money management and financial empowerment."
Canadian Women's Foundation

Acknowledgements

There is a very special circle of influence made up of experts, friends, and family that I engaged with while writing the Savvy Money Gal. I wish to acknowledge them for their inspiration, subject matter expertise, and for helping me to hone and shape my voice.

Julie Salisbury, thank you for publishing my work, seeing the vision of this book, and appreciating the research and insight that anchors it. Your commitment to excellence and passion for your craft is clearly evident. Your team were marvellous to work with and made this journey most memorable.

Patrick, my husband and life partner, thank you for always being there for me with your unwavering strength, love, patience, and encouragement.

Kyle, thank you for being an inspiration in my life. You are the reason I do what I do. Your presence reminds me every day that there is something in this world greater than myself. I adore who you are and the man you are becoming.

Rita, Lily, Aina, Mom, Dad, Craig, Coleman, Cecelia, Krysta, Harry, Julie, Ali, and Rachel, thank you for all your support, love, and encouragement every day. Your coaching, mentoring, advice, sharing of stories, loyalty, and love have given me the strength to make a difference in this world.

Dr. Catherine Comuzzi, thank you for your expertise in Clinical and Behavioural Psychology. I can't express my gratitude enough. Your words of inspiration, wisdom, and knowledge are threads gently woven throughout this book. Thank you for helping me to fully understand how money can be a metaphor for everything in our lives, and that there is nothing more important in a woman's life than standing in her own strength. Your input right from the beginning has been invaluable to me and will be to my readers. They will learn from your expertise and find more financial success and security.

Pattie Lovett-Reid, thank you for being a professional inspiration to me and a role model for women globally. As CTV's Chief Financial Commentator, you are an exemplar in the industry and someone many women can identify with. Your weekly advice on television around money management strategies helps to increase financial literacy and behaviour modification for women, families, and children. Your personal support and encouragement along the way helped me to stay the course and publish this book.

Nina Mazar, thank you for sharing your world-class research on financial literacy and for showing me that financial literacy is not enough. I understand that financial literacy goes well beyond knowledge and numeracy, and only through behavioural facilitation can people embrace healthy new money habits and practices in their search for more financial success and security.

Canadian Women's Foundation, thank you for your commitment to helping women out of poverty and for the work you are doing to strengthen women and children's economic and emotional well-being. Your support for this book is heartfelt and humbling. I hope to do your organization proud by my words and vision to help women find more financial success and security.

Financial Planning Standards Council, thank you for sharing your research and key steps for helping people find a Certified Financial Planner in their community. A financial plan has the power to boost the emotional well-being of people, which will result in greater control of their lives.

Professor Elizabeth Dunn, thank you for sharing with me the research insights from your book Happy Money: The Science of Smarter Spending. Your research will no doubt help my readers engage in more conscious spending to maximize their happiness in the most positive ways.

To my dear and close friends, you know who you are and how much I value our friendship. Thank you for your support for me as I wrote this book and for your input. You are my huggable circle of friends, and when I write about the value of friendship I am writing about you.
Western University, the Richard Ivey School of Business, thank you for showing me how to become a global citizen, and for giving me the tool kit to reach my goals in life.

Contents

Prologue

Who is a Savvy Money Gal?

"Everyone has inside of him a piece of good news. The good news is that you don't know how great you can be! How much you can love! What you can accomplish. And what your potential is!"
Anne Frank (1929-1945) Author

A Savvy Money Gal embraces a winning mindset and looks to the future; she is authentic and lives within her means. She is conscious of her choices and she lives by simple truths and simple luxuries. She is balanced and strives for a clutter-free life. She stands in her own strength and lives with enhanced financial security.

A Savvy Money Gal is someone like you and me.
She lives by a set of values: truth, honesty, kindness, and authenticity. Love, happiness, peace of mind, and her health matter most to her. She lives within this truth. She is joyful. She is authentic, and does not live in fear. She can overcome barriers by exhibiting qualities to get her to where she wants to go.

A Savvy Money Gal is someone who knows who she is and what matters to her.
She knows that harmony is important and is a priority in her life. She knows that life offers trade-offs where choices must be made with her money.

A Savvy Money Gal finds value in simple pleasures or luxuries.
Whether it is a new pair of shoes, a college education, a family home, or global travel, she gets what she wants because she knows where she is today and where she wants to go.

A Savvy Money Gal is grounded and anchored because she has incredible self-belief.
She manages negative thoughts that come into her mind. She is in control. She is authentic and doesn't have to impress anyone. She is driven by her goals, and her spending aligns to the long-term vision she has for herself. She resists temptations when presented to her.

A Savvy Money Gal is self-aware and conscious of the decisions she makes with her life and her money.
She is organized, meaning her life is not in chaos. She is strong, stands in her own strength, and doesn't rely on anyone for her financial security.

Be that Gal!

A Savvy Money Gal is a Global Citizen

To all of you who want to get savvier about your money and get more, this is a book about where you have been, and more importantly where you are going on your road to success. You are embarking on a journey that will without doubt change how you view your money and help you find greater financial security and abundance in your life.

This book offers you a step-by-step process on how to become savvier with your money and how to make better choices. The 6 Savvy Money Gal Strategies are dedicated to women and money, and offer readily available strategies within your reach. Learning about yourself can be scary. I learned a lot about myself in writing this book and hope you will embrace the deep insight, research and strategies about money that have redefined money for me. I offer you, my reader, a road map of inspiration to help you embrace new beliefs about yourself and your money.

We don't live in a gilded cage. The money we earn and spend operates in a greater context. Personal incomes are not growing the way they used to, and what we do with our money matters more than ever. I want to update you on global trends that are emerging around financial literacy, personal debt and low savings rates, that make life more challenging for each and every one of us. We feel the impact every day.

There are other socio-economic issues we face around cultural mythologies about women, the glass ceiling of money, women in poverty, work life balance challenges, and a new set of unmatched concerns for women as we age around our health, spending, and money. I will keep the facts to a minimum but we can't run and hide from the realities of the world a Savvy Money Gal lives in.

Most of us have heard of the term financial literacy and would agree that increasing our financial literacy results in better choices for ourselves, better financial outcomes and more financial security. For some of us this may mean becoming more knowledgeable about our money and learning new terms. For others it may mean learning about various financial ratios, for example, how compounding interests work and/or the time value of money. You won't find a lot of math equations or problems to solve in this book. Although valuable, our focus will be on helping you overcome bad money habits by embracing new strategies. If you feel you could benefit from increasing your financial literacy skills around numeracy, I recommend you take a financial literacy quiz to learn more about numeracy and money at: www.usfinancialcapability.org/quiz/php. Our focus will be on understanding your emotions, values, behaviours and habits in order to help you recreate and redefine your money today.

And finally, as you begin to recreate yourself and redefine yourself while reading this book, share your new found intrinsic wealth with those around you. As you climb, raise up those around you – women helping women. The more we lift up those around us, the more we will break through the barriers that hold us back.

A Savvy Money Gal Lives by Simple Truths

> *"You can live a lifetime and, at the end of it, know more about other people than you know about yourself."*
> **Beryl Markham (1902-1986) Aviator**

This quote by Beryl Markham is powerful and reminds me of the importance of understanding myself, being true to who I am and never losing focus about what I value most in my life. I hope it makes you think about your life by asking yourself a few questions:

- How well do I know myself?
- What do I value in my life?
- Where do I want to go in life?
- What if anything is holding me back?

A Savvy Money Gal wants more in her life but, until now, figuring out the meaning of "more" has been daunting.

As we begin our journey, I want you to keep the questions I just mentioned top of mind. Most of us have little time to do the things we need to get done, let alone spend time thinking about our lives. What if I told you that learning more about yourself and your money values would help you get more financial security and more of what you want out of life? I am not going to ask you to choose between need and want, because both are achievable. What I am offering to you, my reader, is the opportunity to spend some quality time on learning about yourself, your values, where you are in life, and how to get to where you want to go. Wouldn't you agree you are worth this investment?

> *"Women who are confident of their abilities are more likely to succeed than those who lack confidence, even though the latter may be much more competent, talented and industrious."*
> **Joyce Brothers (1927-2013) American Psychologist**

A Savvy Money Gal loves to learn more about herself.

This book is a journey of self-discovery where you will begin to increase your awareness about your life and what you do with your money. To get you on the right footing, I want to provide you with a simple but effective framework to think about. There are no rules in this book or lists of 100+ things to do. There are only 6 strategies that will redefine your life. The Savvy Money Gal framework does not need to be memorized because it is the underlying current in this book. But what I want you to think about is making better choices for yourself and finding more financial security. Embracing the 3 C's of a Savvy Money Gal- Clarity, Confidence, and Control- are the pillars of our journey together. When you bring together the 3 C's something pretty powerful happens that will ready you for more financial security. It goes something like this...

- A Savvy Money Gal understands herself, her values, and has increased consciousness (mindfulness) about everything including her money.

- A Savvy Money Gal has deeper personal insight. With this awareness, comes a clear picture or vision she has for her life.

- A Savvy Money Gal is empowered and self-confident. She is in control of her future and her choices, and has more options. She makes informed and good decisions and doesn't second guess herself.

- A Savvy Money Gal makes fact-based decisions about her life that are informed. She is knowledgeable, and when she doesn't know something (which is rare) she knows who to turn to. She works hard and her money is working for her, like never before.

- A Savvy Money Gal is in control of her life. Her money gets her what she wants, because what she wants is what she needs.

The Power of Clarity, Confidence and Control

> *"Success breeds confidence."*
> **Beryl Markham (1902 – 1986) Aviator**

Clarity

A Savvy Money Gal knows who she is and what she wants. She is authentic and lives a life of meaning and purpose.

Confidence

A Savvy Money Gal feels good everyday. She knows where she is going and feels good about her choices and decisions.

Control

A Savvy Money Gal is in charge of her life and her money. She is strong, informed, and makes savvy decisions.

> *"Knowledge alters what we seek as well as what we find."*
> **Freda Adler (1934-) Criminologist**

A Savvy Money Gal knows deep down in her heart that she could improve her money management strategies.

Juggling your daily demands exhausts all of your energy. At the end of the day, your head crashes on your pillow until the next day, when you get up and do it all over again. I get that. And if this isn't enough, women encounter a daily myriad of mixed messages about how we should be living our lives. Everyone seems to have an opinion. But we know we could be doing better with ourselves and with our money. We search for more.

A Savvy Money Gal is not unhappy in her life.
She knows she could be getting more out of her life and her money. Yet, she no longer sacrifices her own personal happiness for the sake of others, and has balance and clarity on how she spends her time.

A Savvy Money Gal embraces her own beauty and the beauty around her.
As I sit in my office in downtown Vancouver and look at amazement and wonder at the beauty that surrounds me, I ask myself a simple question. What is the promise I want to make to my reader to find the ability to embrace the 6 Savvy Money Gal strategies? Will I help you to find more love, happiness, peace of mind, and take better care of yourself? Will you see yourself more clearly and will you embrace the idea of being a Savvy Money Gal?

Deep in my heart, I know I can make a difference in your life. I want to make a difference in a way that gives you more financial security and abundance, and boosts your emotional well-being. Feeling good about yourself, your life and how your money is working for you will give you a boost.

$$\boxed{\text{Happiness + Energy + Power = Financial Security}}$$

A Savvy Money Gal must manage her financial resources as never before.
As you become more aware of yourself while reading this book, you will begin to make more mindful decisions with your money. As you get more control over your thoughts, feelings and emotions, you will gain more control over your happiness and health. You will learn to derive more value and more happiness from your money. By being present with your thoughts and living in the moment, you will begin to find an authenticity that will empower you. My goal is to help you become more balanced, mindful, and conscious of the choices you are making with your money every day of your life.

How I Became a Savvy Money Gal

I became a Savvy Money Gal when I developed an ability to tune out the extraneous noise around me. I found it was easier to let go of the past; including bad money management strategies and create new money habits. I discovered that I was able to embark on a journey to enhance my life and settle my mindset surrounding the concepts of financial security and abundance. I use the term "financial security" to mean financial security and abundance as a state of mind in which head, heart, and money are in harmony. Much like Dorothy in the Wizard of Oz who always had the power to go home, I was born with the power to create a life of meaning and purpose just like everyone else is. I just needed to find my way. When you learn to embrace new savvy money strategies, you will stand in your own strength and find more financial security. Each of us will arrive at this stage when the moment is right.

Savvy Money Gal Financial Services Consulting

Savvy Money Gal (www.savvymoneygal.com) is a financial services consulting business through which I help individuals get on the path to financial success through personal one-on-one money and life coaching. I offer a full suite of tools and resources designed to help women save more money, make more money doing what they love, budget and create spending plans, and set and achieve personal goals. My skills based learning programs are grounded in best practices and reflect insight and application of leading edge research and knowledge. I also help financial service organizations increase client loyalty through conducting "women and money" workshops, and advising on "women and money" strategies.

Through Savvy Money Gal, I offer skill-based learning to help women solve money challenges by getting to the root cause of what is holding them back. Women are facing challenging money decisions daily that can have a significant impact on their lives. I help women like you better understand their values, emotions, behaviours, and habits in the quest to find more financial security.

Savvy Money Gal offers over thirty six blog articles on women and money, free online tools and resources, workshops in North America, and keynote speaking engagements, to help women become exemplars in managing money. We refer to well respected companies to offer holistic and comprehensive solutions for women, including debt and credit counselling, professional organizing, financial planning, investment advising, and will and estate planning.

> *"The foolish seek happiness over the horizon.*
> *The wise find it under their feet."*
> **Anonymous**

All my best,
Anita

P.S. "The future belongs to those who believe in their dreams." Eleanor Roosevelt (1884-1962) Former First Lady of the United States

Introduction

Our First Steps

"My heart is singing for joy this morning. A miracle has happened! The light of understanding has shone upon my little pupil's mind, and behold, all things are changed."
Anne Sullivan (1866-1936) American Educator of the Blind and Deaf

Before we get to the heart of this book, I want to cover some important things. Each chapter will begin with an inspiring quote intended to get you thinking about your life, your money, and about what the chapter will unfold. We will also start each chapter with positive affirmations. Each of the 6 Savvy Money Gal Strategies will offer a personal learning goal. The goals will be very tangible and well within your reach. The intent is to teach you skills that will help you transform your life. I will also share with you some leading research just to add a little more strength to our discussion.

A Savvy Money Gal starts with the end results in mind.
She is organized and methodical. She does not engage in random thoughtless activities. She is focused and is guided by her vision for herself; defined by the goals she sets and achieves.

A Savvy Money Gal has experienced life's ups and downs.
All of us share a common bond of money stories that we have experienced and, I hope, have overcome. I will share with you money stories of remarkable gals who have overcome obstacles and challenges that ordinarily would stop most of us in our tracks. You will learn about her journey, her pain and how she has become savvier with her money.

  I hope you can relate to each and every story, because you may find yourself somewhere in this book. After each chapter, I will present you with some guided exercises and a touch point. Concurrently, I will ask you to set aside some of your sacred time each week to focus on yourself and your money. This time has to be sacred and only for you. It is so easy to give up our time for other demands in life, but in order to get the most out of this book I suggest that you block off time each week. If you don't commit to this priority, someone else will steal your time for their priorities. Own your calendar; own how you spend your time.

The Savvy Money Gal follows a predictable and consistent pattern in her life.
To recap, our journey together will follow a path guided by:

- An inspiring quote intended to get you thinking about your life
- A personal skills-based learning goal to help guide our activities together
- A remarkable story of a woman who has overcome a challenge in her life
- Factoids or research insights to help strengthen our discussion
- A guided exercise to reinforce our new skills
- And finally, a quick hello from me to see how you are doing

It's that simple. You may find yourself wondering, at times, where we are going and whether to stay the course. Stay the course. Trust the process. Trust yourself. You will find inner strength, courage, and conviction to do things differently and transform into a new and better person when it comes to your money. Ultimately, you will learn to embrace the 6 Savvy Money Gal strategies, take charge of your future, and get the life you want and so deserve.

Savvy Step #1: Personal Pledge

A Savvy Money Gal commits 100% to any task or activity she does.
The first thing to do is make a Personal Pledge to yourself that you want to go on this journey, that you will commit to your personal pledge, and finish the journey. It is also very important that you set aside some time for yourself.

I, _____, pledge to honour myself by taking a journey of self-discovery in order to improve how I manage my money. I pledge to read this book and to engage in the short exercises and guided questions. Dated this day_____, month_____, and year_____.
Signed:_____.

Savvy Step #2: Creating a Personal and Positive Affirmation

A Savvy Money Gal knows the value of positive affirmations.
The second step to take is to create your own personal, positive affirmation. An affirmation is an excellent way not only to visualize success in your life, but to program your mind for change. An affirmation is a short phrase of key words that encompass specific details pertaining to one of your deepest desires or even a cute phrase you have heard and like. By reading or saying your personal affirmation twice daily for the next while, you will actually start programming yourself to achieve it.

Remember the cute tale about the little engine that could? The little engine created a personal affirmation: "I think I can. I think I can." Creating your own personal affirmation is similar to this. Create a secret phrase now that will inspire you to move forward each and every day. It could be something as simple as "Go Girl. Go Girl." Have fun. Personal finance can be so dry and uninteresting, so any chance you and I get to have some fun, let's go for it. My personal affirmation is: "This girl is on fire." I use this phrase to remind myself that anything is possible in life and that I have the ability to get what I want. It acts as a source of inner strength, courage, and conviction, and gives me the wind beneath my wings. It's the same thing as standing in my own strength.

When you feel self-doubt or find yourself blocked, repeat your affirmation to yourself to get you over any bump or difficult situation. Later, when you become more confident about your money and start making improved choices, your positive affirmation may change. That's great. The point here is to be nice to yourself and use a positive affirmation as a symbol, or reminder, of how wonderfully gifted you are. Celebrate yourself.

Savvy Step #3: Making Your Money a Priority

A Savvy Money Gal makes her money a priority.

The third step to take is to honour yourself and give yourself time to read this book and practice the strategies. By making your money a priority you will gain more control over it and will learn to overcome bad money habits. With hard work, perseverance, and commitment, you can accomplish a great deal. Please mark time off on your calendar. When the going gets tough and life demands increase, do not give away your sacred learning time.

The most important thing you can do for yourself is to dedicate time and energy to uncovering ways to improve your money management strategies. Personally, I set aside one hour every Friday to work on my financial priorities. I call it Personal Finance Friday. I spend time on keeping my money life organized and planning my future. It's empowering. The moment you give away this sacred time is the moment you relinquish control of your money. It will no longer be a priority in your life. Getting a handle on your money and developing improved money management strategies will empower you in all areas of your life. So please keep this time sacred.

The sacred weekly time is an important commitment, but you can move through each chapter at your own pace. You may focus on these commitments during weekly sacred time, regardless of your reading progress. It is important to be consistent in how you approach this program; but there is no set time limit on how fast you read through the chapters.

Savvy Step #4: Envisioning Your Future

A Savvy Money Gal can visualize and see her future.

She is goal-focused. The fourth step to take is to engage in self-visualization. Success is a state of mind. Many of you have heard of the power of visualization and how this can act as a force to guide you in the direction you want to go. Some of you may not have tried it or may not be a believer. Trust me when I say it works. As I increasingly utilize the power of visualization, I find it working for me in ways I never imagined. Because when you visualize something you are actually moving into an area of your subconscious and reframing it. You are guiding your thoughts and in turn your behaviour and actions.

Oprah Winfrey uses visualization. She is a firm believer in the power of the subconscious, using positive affirmations and having a goal-centered approach to life. She creates vision boards for herself to help guide her on her life journey. Just a little hint: we will be creating a vision board too!

> *"The biggest adventure you can take is to live the life of your dreams."*
> **Oprah Winfrey (1954-) Talk Show Host**

Comedian Jim Carrey uses visualization. Defining moments for him were when he had nothing: no job, no money, no home; he started visualizing a different life for himself. He went so far as to write a $10 million dollar cheque to himself. When he had moments of self-doubt- Hollywood is known for rejection- he would engage in positive visualization to overcome self-limiting beliefs. Today, Jim Carrey is a very wealthy man. The point is if you believe it, you will achieve it. Create a mental roadmap for your success.

I practice visualization and meditation daily to help maintain focus on my goals and to squash or manage any negativity in my head. I visualize myself reaching my goals easily and naturally. In fact, I envision my success in whatever I do. I create a mental image and road map that guides my subconscious, an area of ourselves that is often resistant to change. By visualizing your success you will learn to diminish and manage negative thoughts that can hold you back and replace it with positive, guided imagery. I find the entire process liberating and freeing. I focus on the result.

Savvy Step #5: Creating Your Money Diary

A Savvy Money Gal writes in a journal every day.

The fifth step to take is to engage in some creative writing. Here, you can have a lot of fun. As a young girl, perhaps you spent time writing your thoughts in a personal journal. You may still have this habit today. Journaling is a wonderful release that gives you permission to let go of things that you may be keeping in your mind. It's freeing.

> *"I have no riches but my thoughts. Yet these are wealth enough for me."*
> **Sara Teasdale (1884-1933) American Poet**

Create a "money diary" and start writing in it every day. Aim for a minimum of fifteen minutes; add more time if needed or desired. Write about anything that comes to mind about your life and your money. Start thinking of the two being interconnected. Start with an entry about your life first. Then follow with a money entry. An example of an entry could be something like this:

Life: "I was thinking about my life today and some of the friends that I have lost touch with. It seems like yesterday Sandra and I were good friends. Years ago, we spent so much time together, but something went wrong. We lost touch. I wonder what happened to her. Is she married? Does she have children? Is she happy?"

Money: "I received my credit card bill today and I was so elated. I didn't use it once last month. My balance is dwindling. I have two more payments to make and that's it. I can't believe I finally got my spending under control because it has bothered me for some time now."

Or, you might write: "Crap, in a few more days, it is the beginning of the month and my rent is due. I get paid a few days later. Maybe I can ask my landlord to hold off on cashing my cheque because I won't have enough money. If my cheque bounces the bank will charge me and my landlord a bunch of money and fees. Gosh. What should I do? Is there anything I can return to the store that will give me more cash to make my rent? What if I took a cash advance on my credit card, etc. It will be just this one time."

The point is to just write down your thoughts, and not to judge, critique, or evaluate what you write. Putting your money thoughts on paper may cleanse you of related thoughts that might just be caught in your head and have no place to go. Writing down your thoughts provides you with an outlet and often many of us feel better when we express our inner feelings. It can be freeing. Dedicate a journal right now for your daily thoughts.

A Savvy Money Gal embraces positive energy and shuns away from negativity.
If you want to go one step further, and this is optional, try recording or writing down negative

words or phrases that come to mind in your daily life. Toss them out of the window, in the garbage, or on the floor. Let this be a reminder to you that negativity and self-doubt have no room in your life. The goal here is to start replacing negative thoughts with ones that are more positive and uplifting. Sometimes words can hold us back from moving forward. People can also hold us back from where we want to go. I will share with you some easy to use strategies on how to manage these people and the impact they can have in your life. I always keep in mind a famous saying by Eleanor Roosevelt: "no one can make you feel inferior without your consent."

> *"Learn from the past, set vivid, detailed goals for the future, and live inthe only moment of time of which you have control, now."*
> **Denis Waitley (1933-) Motivational Speaker**

Exercises

A Savvy Money Gal loves to learn and increase her skill set.
Short, guided exercises that follow each chapter will help you embrace the 6 Savvy Money Gal strategies. Each exercise is intended to help you acquire and practice new skills and reinforces the material presented in the chapter.

These exercises are designed to help you to better connect with your thoughts and feelings about your money. They will reinforce some of the key points we have discussed. My approach will be to encourage you to overcome any personal money problems or challenges by engaging in learning exercises that will stretch your thinking and heighten your understanding of issues that are relevant. I will not attempt to educate you; rather I will guide and inform you. You may have some healthy scepticism along the journey. I hope so, because many of you will have tried to overcome bad money habits before and it didn't work. As you engage in the exercises, please focus on yourself and not on others around you. Remember, those around you may release some subtle sabotage to hold you back. Other people's plans are not your plans. Remember this. These lessons will eventually result in your transformation and facilitate your quest to find more joy and happiness in your life. It may be preferable to complete exercises in privacy, in a quiet place where you can be alone.

Skill-based learning programs, which is what this book offers, require a little more effort on your part. I challenge you to stay the course. Change is difficult for all of us, but if you can commit to your learning, you will grow and get more out of your life and your money.

Connecting with You

> *"The important thing is that when you come to understand some-*
> *thing, you act on it, no matter how small that act is. Eventually*
> *it will take you where you need to go."*
> **Sister Helen Prejean (1939-) Activist**

A Savvy Money Gal loves to share her ideas and talk about her life.

There is one final thing I want to share with you. Because I am not in front of you to chat or to see how you are progressing through this book, I am going to ask you a few questions at the end of each chapter. The questions are different from the exercises. As you become more comfortable connecting with me through this book, you will probably notice how your responses change according to the questions I ask you. I hope your responses evolve beneficially. The ultimate goal is to develop positive changes surrounding how you view and manage your life and money. If you get stuck or stumble, reach out to me at info@savvymoneygal.

Getting from Point A to Point B with the Six Savvy Money Strategies

Let's begin our journey by looking at where you are today and where we are going. I want to take you on a journey from Point A to Point B. For each of us, our starting point may be different, based on where we are in our lives. However, the journey we will embark on is one of shifting your mindset away from behaviors, attitudes, and beliefs that might be holding you back or keeping you stuck, to more positive, energy-based behaviors that will result in better financial outcomes. Below, I created two word clouds to show you some of the thoughts or feelings you may have today that are probably holding you back from finding more financial success and security. Circle the words that may apply to you. Then, on the right side of the page, circle all the words or phrases that feel right to you. Let's focus on getting you from Point A to Point B.

> *"Chains of habit are too light to be felt until they are too heavy to be broken."*
> **Warren Buffett (1930-) CEO**

From Point A	⇨	To Point B:

From Point A	To Point B:
Not doing anything	Being motivated to make changes
Avoiding	Expressing feelings openly
Denying	Managing negative thoughts and worry
Lacking self-belief	Looking forward, not backward
Repeating past money mistakes	Knowing problems can be solved
Being consumed by a life transition	Knowing what matters
Having poorly defined life priorities	Be conscious of the past, live in the present
Being consumed by negative thoughts	Being aware of the reality
Spending mindlessly	Making conscious and mindlful choices
Having too much debt	Living more authentically
Living an unaffordable lifestyle	Saving more money
Buying now, paying later attitude	Spending wisely
Being caught in a vicious credit cycle	Having long-term visions and goals
Paying bills late or interest on credit cards	Living a life that is simplified & organized
Living paycheque to paycheque	Finding joy in simple things
Engaging in impulse or emotional shopping	Seeking professional advice
Making uninformed decisions	Planning ahead
Making fear-based decisions	Balancing the power in relationships
Relying too heavily on others for security	Becoming a role model
Not having a financial plan	Engaging in Financial Planning
Not investing	Learning about investing

Life-Changing Money Strategies

A Savvy Money Gal embraces strategies that will help her put her goals within reach. Each and every one of us has bad money habits. There are plenty of examples: overspending, not saving enough, paying bills late, carrying interest on our credit cards, emotional shopping, impulse shopping, living paycheque to paycheque, distracted spending, or being overwhelmed by spending choices. I suspect you may already know your bad money habits and are avoiding them.

All of us have deep rooted habits. Most of the decisions we make are made in an area of the brain called the subconscious. Many of the decisions we make are not in our consciousness. We don't actually think about a decision before we act. Why? Researchers tell us we are so conditioned by our subconscious that it just takes over our lives. For example, have you ever gone into your car and arrived at your destination and asked yourself, how did I get here? It's a strange experience and no you are not losing your mind, but you have been guided by your subconscious. Bad money habits live in our subconscious as well, and unless we unlock them and replace them with the 6 Savvy Money Gal Strategies we will continue to be guided by old stories that we have outgrown.

I would like to present the 6 Savvy Money Gal Strategies to give you a snapshot of the territory we will be covering as we move toward embracing these life-changing strategies:

The 6 Savvy Money Gal Strategies:

Savvy Money Gal Strategy #1: Adopt a Winning Mindset around Money
Savvy Money Gal Strategy #2: Stop Living in the Past and Look to the Future
Savvy Money Gal Strategy #3: Be Authentic: Don't Live Beyond Your Means
Savvy Money Gal Strategy #4: Be Conscious of Your Life and Money Choices
Savvy Money Gal Strategy #5: Organize Your Life and Money
Savvy Money Gal Strategy #6: Rely on Yourself for Your Financial Security

Savvy Strategy #1: Adopt a Winning Mindset around Money

Having a winning mindset about money is the first step on your journey towards finding financial security. When you embrace a winning mindset, anything is possible. You relinquish self-doubt, self-sabotage, and the feelings of being helpless or stuck in your life. Sometimes it is really hard to control the critical voices in your head, caused by your mind not by your money. Once you manage that nagging voice that unconsciously sabotages your success and how you manage your money, you will start to feel better about the possibilities for your future. But, watch out! Self-doubt may prevent you from making better decisions with your money.

Believing in yourself and having an unwavering inner strength are the essential ingredients to having a winning money mindset. When you believe in yourself, you will become more peaceful, calm, and optimistic about your future. Positive affirmations, mindful meditations, and yoga will assist with your growth.

Rescue yourself from feeling overwhelmed, tired, doubtful, and helpless in your life. For example, you may decide to revisit having a spending plan or budget, and remember the results of your last attempts. You may reflect on why the budget didn't work and push yourself harder to stick to it. Stay the course. Above all, don't get defeated. Forge ahead with self-belief and confidence in your success.

Savvy Strategy #2: Stop Living in the Past and Look to the Future

Some of us may have had a major life transition that derails our life completely. It is hard to recover from these life events. Sometimes old and outdated money values and paradigms that we have carried far too long can accompany these life events. When we live in the past, we bind ourselves to past mistakes, to old money stories. You can't move forward and keep repeating past money mistakes; they keep you a prisoner.

Letting go of the past is the recipe for future success. Therefore, moving away from old values and toward the future will empower you to make good choices with your money grounded in facts. Once you let go of your past and forge a new future for yourself, your money can flow again, and become fresh. For example, you may be carrying an old money habit from a period of your life when you engaged in overspending, suffered an investment loss, or lost money because of a poor money decision. These may have held you back from moving forward some time ago. Releasing these old habits will allow you to believe in your current and future financial success.

Savvy Strategy #3: Be Authentic: Don't Live Beyond Your Means

Each and every one of us has spent money beyond our means. For some of us, this is based upon mistaken ideas that are not proven true in the long term. When we are inauthentic, we engage in a falsehood. It is much like fake friendships: "friends" we don't necessarily like, but are friendly to, just to be nice. In the same way, we have allowed ourselves to use our money to pretend to be something we are not. For example, we use credit cards to live a lifestyle we can't afford in order to impress people we don't necessarily like. We seek status with our pretend money.

Rob a woman of her Gucci handbag and she is naked. Who is she? Many women in this mindset need to stop trying to impress other women and stop hiding behind products to boost their self-esteem. As cited in a research study by Yajin Wang and Vladas Griskevicius, sometimes women try to impress other women with their expensive handbag or some other luxurious product, trying to show off that object as a symbol of their partner's profound love and devotion. When our money becomes authentic like ourselves, we become more conscious about our money choices. We know where it goes and feel real, authentic, and good about ourselves!

Living more authentically is about being real with who you are as a person. When you become real and authentic with yourself, you no longer need to use your money to impress people or seek status, because you are happy with who you are and what you have. When you are authentic with your money, you no longer have anything to prove to anyone. Good enough is enough. You feel real. Life is simple. You are making conscious and mindful choices with your money. You are very present and much more self-aware with your money. You think twice before buying something and you no longer engage in impulse buying nor regret how you spend your money.

Savvy Strategy #4: Be Conscious of Your Life and Money Choices

Nobody is immune to the lure of spending "feel good money"; this is money we spend unconsciously, without paying careful attention to thinking the purchase through. When our hearts are broken and we have been betrayed, we become good friends with "feel good money". Spending money unconsciously helps us fill a void in our life, and compensates for things we avoid talking about; for example, loneliness, rejection, fear, isolation, and insecurity. Some of us engage in extreme unconscious spending sprees, where our compulsions are uncontrollable. We probably should not be spending "feel good money", but we buy things to make ourselves feel better.

There are times when we spend our money to feel worthy or validated, with the sense that "if I appear to have money, people will love me." Spending "feel good money" helps soothe our inner wounds and provides temporary fixes or highs to mask the deep pain we feel. Many people hide behind their money. I know many people who feel more confident driving luxury cars rather than economy cars. They view their car as a status symbol, when in reality they probably could only afford to buy an economy car. Money and power can make people feel better. People who engage in hiding behind money usually do so because they are deeply wounded and hurt in life. Emotional shopping to the extreme can become compulsive shopping when someone goes shopping daily in order to feel better. Unconscious spending of "feel good money" needs to be re-directed into conscious, thoughtful, and aware spending. Loving yourself, honoring yourself, and spending your money in an authentic way protects your money goals so your spending is measured and reasonable.

Savvy Principle #5: Organize your Life and Money

Most of us are feeling distracted in our lives. We are being pulled in so many directions. Who has time to get organized? Most of us feel unorganized. But what if I told you that getting organized with your money will increase your financial security? When our money is disorganized we may find ourselves having too many accounts that we don't really need or use, paying far too much interest, and having no idea how we spend our money. We don't have control over it; it is in charge of our lives. We have no idea where it goes, how to keep more of it, or how to harness it in order to reach our goals. Disorganized money creates a messy life. When our money is not organized it can create hardship, stress, and worry. However, when money becomes organized it gets cleaned up and it becomes clutter-free money.

In essence, money that is managed and directed makes us more money savvy. It is no longer distracting. It is money with a purpose and a clear direction and focus. It never gets squandered or wasted, because its purpose has been fully defined with a clear vision. It is organized and can be easily found and accessed. It is never forgotten or misplaced. Disorganized money often occurs when you are overwhelmed and have little time for yourself. Your calendar is messy and so is your life. Bills may get paid late because you can't find them. Your credit score may have taken a beating and you may have difficulty getting credit. You have too many bank or credit card accounts and an excess of cards in your wallet, making reconciling your money difficult each month.

Savvy Strategy #6: Rely on Yourself for Your Financial Security

All of us have been thoughtless spenders at times, less than mindful of the consequences. Intelligent women can make bad choices. Who hasn't done something with their money they regret? Who hasn't made uninformed decisions with their money resulting in bad results? Who hasn't at some point looked to be rescued by someone in their life? When you believe the government, your partner, or your parents will take care of you, you relinquish control over your future. For example, perhaps you choose not to invest your money because you don't understand the basics, and you don't want to appear unknowledgeable. Maybe you are letting your partner manage your money and have relinquished control. Perhaps you have not taken the proper steps to write a will. Or, could it be that you are not making saving a priority by putting aside at least 10% of your income every year?

When you take control of your future and your money, you become savvy. You feel empowered, and are engaging in economic strength. You are investing money in a way that you never imagined and are engaged in financial planning. Your emotional well-being has sky rocketed, you feel in control, you are confident about your future. When you take control of your financial security, you engage in a new principle of continuous learning. You have become more curious about the world of finance, and you stay informed and knowledgeable about things that matter. You know when to engage experts for advice and you know that you don't need to be alone in your quest for financial security. You are no longer fearful and you worry less.

Is More Money the Answer?

A Savvy Money Gal values her money.
Let's make something very clear from the beginning. Money matters. The desire to make money and to provide for yourself and your family is important. For the single gal, there is no shoulder to lean on. In fact, people who live without much money will tell you their quality of life is less than ideal. Making money is at the heart of living, but what matters even more is what we do with our money. For some, more money is absolutely the answer, particularly if you are finding it difficult to make ends meet. However, for many of us, more money may not be the answer to our money worries or concerns.

For most of us, money is a limited resource or scarce commodity. There never seems to be enough, making saving more challenging. By nature, women are terrific savers. We all want financial security and saving is a clear path to get there. Yet, all of us wish we had more money, because we think having more money is the answer to fixing what is not working with our money. In the end, however, the reality is that more money can often bring a new set of challenges and problems to manage. All in all, the better you manage your money, no matter how much you have, the more control you will have over your money and your life.

A Savvy Money Gal knows that life is full of trade-offs around her choices.
Women are often held back by bad habits or misaligned money strategies. Potential bad money habits are: excessive personal debt, overspending, impulse shopping, paying bills late, not saving

enough, not planning ahead, not being informed about money, having too many credit and debit cards, not saving for a rainy day, not preparing for the unexpected (no insurance), a lack of willpower, not taking responsibility, refusing to be held accountable, high interest rates, the absence of a spending plan or budget, less than defined goals, no joy in saving, relying on others, being lifestyle-focused (instant gratification), living in the past, weak motivation, and ongoing distractions. Do not get overwhelmed by this list of bad habits, by no means am I suggesting that women cannot manage money. It is however important to recognize that when it comes to your money choices, you have to make trade-offs about what to spend on and what to save for, you have to prioritize what is important to you. What I want you to be aware of is that bad money habits can creep up on all of us, and they don't happen overnight.

A Savvy Money Gal keeps her emotions in check.
Women may also be held back by emotions that cause them to feel overwhelmed, angry, tired, disinterested, unprepared, worried, and frustrated, leading to an avoidance of problems and self-sabotage. You get the idea. There are a multitude of influences and bad habits that hold women back. For many of us, our bad habits may originate from self-doubt. Self-doubt can ruminate in our heads for so long that we actually begin to believe it. Ultimately, doubt holds us back and impacts all aspects of our life, affecting how we handle our money.

By nature, women are strong, confident, and nurturing, but not always with their money. We have wonderful gifts to give to those we care about. We never say no and we often take on more than we can handle. Yet, for some reason, we let the pessimistic voices run rampant in our minds, especially with our money choices. We often self-diminish, because of negativity, causing us to make bad decisions. As a result, many of us have acquired an unhealthy disrespect for our money. We blame our money situation and sometimes others for not getting what we need or want. Or, inevitably, we blame the economy, work demands, and lack of balance in our lives, as reasons why we are not getting what we want.

A Savvy Money Gal believes good can be good enough.
When you let go of trying to be perfect and accept that "good enough is good enough", you will begin to prepare yourself to face your bad money habits head on. You won't ignore them but will actively seek to overcome them and turn them into good money habits, creating more success for yourself. Disappointment may emerge when you create unrealistic expectations for yourself and your money. Many women have acquired the insane idea that we have to be perfect at everything we do and that "enough is never enough". These unrealistic, self-imposed attitudes are transferred over to our money, where we feel we never have enough or that making and accumulating money is not okay.

A Savvy Money Gal engages in creative problem solving to understand why money problems exist and how to overcome them once and for all.

For example, a debt consolidation loan may fix a problem of too much debt, but does it really get to the root cause of what drove someone to overspend in the first place? Impulse buying may waste a lot of money and women may spend frivolously on things that really don't matter much, such as expensive makeup. It may make you feel good temporarily, but what value does a $40 eye shadow really have? For some this may be an extreme example; for others a common one. Inevitably, bad money habits are a result of bad money choices. Sometimes bad choices are ill-informed choices, you don't really know better. You may think that keeping a large balance in your savings account is a good money habit. Saving is a good habit that may become a bad habit if you are not also engaged in investing your money, by sending it out to work for you. We all know old habits die hard and many of us are holding on to ones that are no longer relevant; for some reason, we just can't seem to let go of them.

A Savvy Money Gal embraces life's challenges.

Many of us want to ignore our problems because we secretly hope that will make them to go away. All the same, the dirty little secret is that money problems rarely go away on their own, unless you address them and manage the root causes. You can wish all you want, sprinkle magic money fairy dust, or pray for your Prince Charming to arrive, but unless you take control and make your money a priority, you will continue to stare your bad habits in the face when you have, in fact, outgrown them and need to move on. Comparable to having the same hairstyle or makeup for the past ten years, is it not time to change your money style? If your money choices are not working, it is time to change them.

A Savvy Money Gal is rational and makes mindful and conscious choices.

Research tells us that many people fall into predictable patterns of behavior regarding money. You might know what I am referring to. Many of us make the same mistakes over and over again until a cycle gets broken. For example, we might create a spending plan or budget and abandon it soon after, because the results are not immediate. In essence, if we were consistently rational in our behavior and choices, there wouldn't be many money problems. As human beings, however, we are not always consistently rational in our behavior and we may make emotional choices that are less than ideal, especially financial ones. Sometimes it is a matter of not knowing better. Sometimes, we self-sabotage, because we don't believe deep down inside we deserve to be successful. These unwise choices hold us back from finding true financial security. In fact, financial security is not a farfetched concept or idea. Financial security reflects each and every woman's desire to get more from her money and find more joy and happiness. Let's break our old or bad habits and change behavior that is no longer working for us!

Chapter One ~ Strategy #1
Adopt a Winning Mindset around Money

"You have to have confidence in your ability, and then be tough enough to follow through."
Rosalyn Carter (1927 –) Former First Lady of the United States

Personal Learning Goal

As we begin the work of transforming your bad money habits into good money habits, you will first learn skills that will help you adopt a winning mindset around money. Having a winning mindset for anything you pursue in life is a must. To embrace a winning mindset, clear your mind of messages that are no longer working for you or are holding you back. It is amazing how negative messages have a way of staying in our heads far too long, to the point where we begin to believe them. These messages contribute to holding you back or lead to emotions of feeling frazzled, overwhelmed, doubtful, tired, stuck, or helpless. These self-sabotaging feelings and emotions may have blocked your self-confidence in the past and can actually set you up to fail.

When we don't embrace a winning mindset in our lives, our money can become lifeless and lack direction. When we become stuck in life it is because we are holding on to old paradigms, thoughts and messages. Our mindset is programmed during our childhood and if you did not learn the right foundational pieces, you may be living your parents' bad money habits today. If you live with self-doubt, you know how debilitating this can be also. The reality is that if you feel unsure or doubtful, you are not alone. Many women have self-doubt. Many men have self-doubt. It is how you manage self-doubt that can really make a difference.

You can't completely eliminate negative thoughts from the mind, but the ongoing efforts to keep those thoughts at bay serves to keep you real and focused.

Money Story: Carol

Carol grew up in a typical middle class family in the 80s, with her two older brothers and one younger sister. She grew up in a fairly traditional family, where her father worked and her mother stayed at home with the four children until they were school age, upon which time she returned to work to earn money to help pay for family activities, sports, and programs.

Carol's mother was very loving and kind, but she was extremely critical of Carol and her sister; nothing was ever good enough. Carol's mother's need for perfection had a negative impact on Carol and her sister. Carol, who is now in her mid-thirties, recalls how critical her mother was growing up, and believes much of this eroded her self-belief and confidence. She continues to struggle with limiting beliefs today.

If you were to meet Carol, you would think she has it all together, but deep down inside she is highly insecure and uncertain about herself. Carol struggles with feelings of self-doubt daily, but is learning to manage them through the use of positive affirmations, positive visualization, and yoga. She recalls past money decisions or choices that have held her back from achieving financial success; she used to spend her money on personal items to help fill the void she had inside. Although today she is very successful in life and has overcome some of her bad money habits, she admits that she has to manage her negative thoughts daily. "They never really go away," she says. However, she has been able to find more inner peace and acceptance, and healthier attitudes toward her money through daily diligence.

Dr. Catherine Comuzzi, Ed. D Cg Psychology, Psychotherapist, and Master Coach Trainer, notes that "Carol is a classic example of stuck habits. Our relationship to money is one of the strongest life metaphors that reflect our frozen beliefs about ourselves and our capacities. When we pursue a focused examination of these automatic habits and begin to challenge and change the entrenched beliefs and patterns that grip us, we can open to more personal freedom. We women must de-clutter our minds of the negative attitudes we have towards money, to become more mindful of money decisions, and to use money effectively to achieve personal goals."

Many women will sabotage personal success by listening to the nagging voice in the back of their heads. Words can set our expectations and create our beliefs, which may not be true. Words have the ability to shut us down in such a harmful way that it keeps us stuck. Most people are far more fearful of success than they are of failure, primarily because they believe they are not worthy of success. A lack of confidence has deep roots in childhood, and is probably one of the biggest obstacles a woman needs to overcome. Words define our lives, set our expectations, and often do unconsciously sabotage our own success by shutting us down.

When the past speaks with a voice of doom and gloom, the present and future voices of optimism and self-belief are silent. They are silent voices. And silent voices never get heard. When we live in the past, we deny ourselves opportunities for personal growth, and we slow down or impede the realization of our life's dreams.

When we relinquish control of our lives and our money, we wander aimlessly, undirected, in circles, looking for guidance or a beacon to show us the way.

Starting out, women may have a vision for their future, but may not have the economic resources yet to fulfill their goals. Women transitioning to retirement may feel angst as well. All of this creates a level of uncertainty. When you are consumed with thoughts about your future, and are questioning yourself, you have greater difficulty managing self-doubt.

For example, perhaps you created a spending plan or budget in the past only to find after a very short time that you were not getting the results you wanted. You abandoned it. Later, you contemplate trying your budget again and reflect on your past "failure" and say to yourself "no, spending plans don't work. They are useless." Here is where you need to really manage the self-sabotaging behavior. Much like dieting, spending plans are often abandoned because results don't come quickly enough and the restrictive feelings they give you feel disempowering at times.

Confidence Booster
Chase away negative thoughts. Replace them with empowering thoughts or words. Be kind to yourself. Eliminate the word "can't" from your mind.

How to Embrace a Winning Mindset

Having a winning mindset is within your reach. It starts with embracing a life-long pledge to be nice to yourself. It incorporates the ongoing, daily practice of being mindful of your thoughts. It means practicing self-care by reinforcing yourself with self-generated positive thoughts, feelings, and attitudes. This means not letting the negative, unkind, or thoughtless actions of others enter your mind. The kinder or more soulful you become to yourself, the more likely you are to engage in activities that have good outcomes.

It is crucial that you do not use your money in a manner to calm your negative thoughts, feelings, and emotions. Take control of your thoughts, feelings, and emotions by becoming more self-aware, mindful, and living in the moment. Do not take the words and actions of others personally; do not let insecurities set up residence in your head. If you practice standing in your own strength, you will always use your money with more confidence and less fear. You will no longer use it in a way that can self-sabotage you, because you are kind to yourself first, before you are kind to others. You cannot afford to put yourself last when it comes to self-care. You have to be present, mindful, and observant at all times, this is key. If you need to, find a quiet corner and start to breathe and center yourself the minute you notice yourself becoming anxious. Perhaps also divert yourself by repeating one or more of your favourite affirmations. At all times, be proactive the minute you notice unconstructive thoughts surfacing. This ongoing and daily practice will lead to you using your money soulfully, and this is imperative to becoming financially stable and secure, regardless of the amount of income you have coming in at any given time.

When you embrace a winning mindset, you direct your money to manifest a positive attitude that always sees the world for its possibilities, not its flaws. You become more optimistic creating a winning mindset. This winning mindset becomes an unstoppable force in your life.

Break Free to be Yourself and...Never Let Anyone Hold You Back

It is important for all of us to fight against the "glass ceiling" in our lives, the glass ceiling that prevents our growth and advancement. The "glass ceiling" is representative of the barriers we as women face in furthering our goals.

What is the "Glass Ceiling"?

According to the US Department of Labour's fact-finding report of the Federal Glass Ceiling Commission, the phrase glass ceiling "first entered America's public conversation in 1986 when the Wall Street Journal's 'Corporate Woman' column identified a puzzling new phenomenon...an invisible – but impenetrable – barrier between women and the executive suite, preventing them from reaching the highest levels of the business regardless of their accomplishments and merits." It became a metaphor in popular culture. It is important to note that we can subconsciously create our own glass ceiling. There is one created in our societal environment and one created in our own heads by lack of self belief.

Challenge Your Self-Perceptions

There are times in our lives when we encounter people who do not want to see us grow because it makes them very uncomfortable. Change is scary and as you continue down this journey of self-discovery you will change, and others around you will notice the difference. Letting go of your old self-perceptions is difficult; and others will be faced with the same challenge of seeing you in a new light. With change comes the reevaluation of everything in your life – your friends, your job, and your future.

> "I've seen very, very bright women. I use the example of Katherine Graham. ... While she was CEO of the Washington Post, the stock went up [by a lot]. She won a Pulitzer Prize. But she'd been told by her mother, she'd been told by her husband, she'd been told by lots of people that women weren't as good as men in business. It was nonsense. And I kept telling her, you know, 'Quit looking at that fun house mirror. You know, here's a real mirror. You're something.' And as smart as she was, as high grade as she was, you know, as famous as she became, right to her dying day...she had that little voice inside her that kept repeating what her mother had told her a long time ago. So everybody should get a chance to live up to their potential. And women should not hold themselves back. And nobody should hold them back. And that's my message."
> **Warren Buffett (1930-) CEO**

In order to move forward in their own strength and to never let anyone hold them back, women must accept the challenge to retire their old self-perceptions. They must be willing to go out on a limb and create new perceptions and attitudes around their money and their lives. Old paradigms or modelling male behaviours will not work well in the long run; enough women have tried those routes and found that they are dead ends. A woman may want to change and know the change is good, but she may self-sabotage herself. She may attempt to change and one small set-back or failure will defeat her, and she will revert back to the status quo. The most important attributes for any woman to possess are self-awareness and self-confidence. Women need to guard these attributes like fierce lions and never allow anyone, by holding them back, to diminish their self-awareness or self-confidence. To do this, women have to be present, mindful, and standing in their strength on a daily basis, while challenging any negativity as it arises in their minds. There is nobody who can do this for women; they must do this for themselves.

A Savvy Money Gal chooses her friends wisely.

Many women are in relationships with people who don't want to see them grow. Why? When someone changes or grows, it can upset the apple cart. When you start to stand in your own strength and retire your old self-perceptions, others may become jealous or insecure. Your changes may threaten and challenge the status quo. Your newfound inner strength may secretly express that they want the "old you" back. Your friends, partner, or other people in your life may not openly embrace the "new you". People close to you may sabotage your success. The reality is these people are blocked themselves. They may cling to the past to avoid growing or changing. Our close circle of friends must fill us up with joy and happiness, not drain us of our energy.

It is perfectly acceptable to upset the apple cart. Be mindful that YOU are changing and others may not be. Watch out, some people don't embrace change and may try to hold you back. Keep loving them, but stand in your own strength! You may find yourself wanting to expand your friendship circle, because you have outgrown who you were.

A Savvy Money Gal values the power of friendships.

Friends have always been important in this ever-changing world. There are many different types of friends, including those you spend time with, enjoy their company, but do not lean on for emotional support. These are friends that you may share many mutually enjoyable activities with, but everyone likes to keep it light. These friends may be very fond of you, but they look to you for fun, not to comfort you when you are going through challenging times. These friends are likely to disappear when the weather is not fair. At the same time, your fair-weather friends may not expect you to be there when the going gets tough for them either. These are sunny day friendships; there is a place for these friends in your life.

You may meet many interesting people through associating with fair weather friends and sometimes find a new long-time friend along the way.

Then there are the huggable friends, your Go-To gals. These gals are the ones who are always there for you and never judge you for who you are. These are friends who want to be emotionally available for you and enjoy deeper relationships; those who will seek you out for emotional support and advice, and expect to receive the same in return. These friends will tell you when they think you are going off track and when they think you are wrong. Your values may fully align and your money values are probably similar.

If you don't have a lot of friends today, make new ones. One way to make new friends is not to shy away from interacting with fair weather friends, who may be temporary, but broaden your horizons. It may be wise to not expect too much; enjoy what a wide variety of people have to offer. I have lived in three cities in a very short time and have found the key to making new friends in new communities is to be bold and put yourself out there. Stay connected with your old friends, especially the gals who fill you up with positive energy, and those who don't drain you of your goodness. Your friendships will last a lifetime, if you work hard to make this so. A lot of other situations will come and go, but your friends may stand the test of time. Keep your circle of friends close – emotionally and geographically. You can move to the other side of the country, but stay connected. This is easier than ever before with newly available technology.

Creating a Circle That Feels Right

A Savvy Money Gal has a close circle of trusted friends.
As we discussed above, friends matter and can be a terrific support system. Today, many of us are so busy with our lives that we have lost touch with one of the most important aspects of our lives: friendship. Turning to friends can help you weather storms. With an ear to bend, life becomes less confusing, and a good listener will allow you to talk through your options and make better choices for yourself. Sometimes it is really hard to decide upon a course of action without talking it out with someone you trust. There is nothing more powerful than having a chat with one of your closest girlfriends, particularly in a time of need. Our friendships can lift us in ways money can't.

So why talk about friendship in this chapter on adopting a winning mindset? Well, as I was thinking about the conscious use of money, I thought about the times in my life when I felt low or sad. Instead of picking up my purse and wallet to go shopping to fill a void, I picked up the phone to engage one of my friends in conversation to talk through what was bothering me. It has always been my practice to seek support from my sisters, or a close friend, when I find myself in a bit of a jam. This practice has worked well for me.

My circle of friends has shrunk over the years, because my values and life circumstances have changed. My circle reflects who I am today. The circle is small but rich. I have always believed that having a small circle is much more powerful than having too many fair weather friends. However, as discussed earlier, there is definitely a place for fair weather friends and they can be a great source of new friends if you have recently moved to a new community. We all have acquaintances, people we always smile at and say hello to in the workplace and in our neighbourhood, and even some folks we hug regularly, because it gives us all a boost. At the same time, there are others we are more distant with. The main point here is to never cut yourself off from exploring all options to seek out and add to your circle of friends.

In the exercise that follows, we will be focusing on your special circle of true friends, those friends that are always there for you in time of need. These are Go-To friends, the ones with whom we share the most personal things about ourselves; the friends who make us feel safe and secure. Think about the friends who are in your life today and how your circle has changed over the years. Ask yourself the following:

1. Who is in my life and why?

_____

_____

2. Am I creating the right circle of friends for myself and my life as it is now?

_____

_____

3. Who are my Go-To friends?

_____

_____

4. What, or who, is missing in my circle of friends?

_____

_____

Let the answers to these questions inform you, guide you, and provide clarity as you expand and develop strong and healthy friendships.

The Power of Positive Thinking

A Savvy Money Gal views her world positively.
Let's shift gears a little and get back to how to go about creating a winning mindset. Let's think about circumstances in your life, in terms of filling up a cup of water and asking yourself this question: "Is my cup half full or half empty?" This is a terrific question and one I am sure you have heard before. How do you view your life? If you see your cup as half full, you are considered an optimist. If you see your cup as half empty, you tend to be more pessimistic. In life, we are presented with choices. You may opt to have a pessimist's view and live a self-defeated life. Or you may decide to take the optimist's route and link yourself to a positive and good morale; to academic, athletic, military, occupational, and political success; to popularity; to good health; and even to long life and freedom from trauma.

Optimism can be learned. Optimists are confronted with the same hard knocks in this world as pessimists. What differs is the way they explain their misfortune to themselves. Pessimists believe that bad events will last a long time and undermine everything they do. Optimists choose to believe that defeat is just a temporary setback. Rather than dwell on the obstacle or problem and allow themselves to think negative thoughts- for instance "things will never get better" or "if I fail now it will happen again"- optimists use positive reinterpretation. In other words, they reinterpret a negative experience in a way that helps them learn and grow. They view life events as experiences to learn, grow and make better choices in the future. Failure is a way of recalibrating and re-strategizing. Many people will allow failure to define them and keep them stuck. Optimists are unfazed by bad situations; they perceive them as challenges and try harder. If they fall, they simply get back up. Optimists tend to be mindful, live in the moment, and practice self-awareness. They are also less dependent on others for their happiness.

Optimists typically maintain higher levels of emotional well-being during times of stress. Steven Covey in his book, The 7 Habits of Highly Effective People, discusses the importance of maintaining emotional bank accounts with people we care about. When we regularly deposit into the back account with the person we care about, we strengthen the relationship. When you have high emotional well-being and the account is full of deposits, then you can make a withdrawal when needed and your relationship will not suffer. However, if your emotional well-being account is empty due to lack of deposits by you or the other person, and something stressful happens that requires a withdrawal, there is nothing to draw on to help you get grounded. Both you and the other person in your relationship, whether it be a friend or family member, needs to make regular deposits to keep both your levels of emotional well-being high.

Pessimists are likely to react to stressful events by denying that they exist or by avoiding dealing with problems. Pessimists are more likely to quit trying when difficulties arise. Optimists persevere. They don't give up easily. They are known for their patience. Optimists don't assume their goals will be achieved overnight, but that doesn't mean they give up. They continue to inch their way, one step at a time, closer to their goals and dreams. Optimists are healthier and live longer.

A Savvy Money Gal never underestimates the power of positive thinking, nor does she allow herself to wallow in pessimism or negative thinking.
Positive thinking helps with clarity, confidence and control. It is a useful strategy to remain serene, peaceful, calm, and energetic.

Maintaining Inner Calm and Balance Regardless of Any Random Intrusions

Put simply, balance your life and you will balance your financial situation. How is this possible? When your life is in overload, as happens to everyone from time to time, you may find yourself neglecting your self-care and forgetting to utilize all your strategies for remaining soulful with your life and your money. You may find yourself slipping into self-doubt, when you are feeling tired, frazzled, and overwhelmed. You may not be functioning at an optimal level because your energy levels have become too low and you've become bogged down in negative thinking. These are the times when you have to double your efforts to stay in the moment, pay attention, be mindful, and remain self-aware. The sooner you are able to return to inner calm and balance, the less money you may spend on convenience items, impulse purchases, or emotional shopping. Let's explore this further.

Your thoughts can't hold any power over you. If you notice yourself flooded by negative thoughts, detach from them and let them go. As discussed earlier, you may have to find a quiet corner and do some breathing and affirmations. You may have to spend a few minutes calming yourself down as you would an upset child. Take this time to be kind and loving to yourself and remember that you need to nip the negative voices in the bud, before it starts to take over your mind. Negative thinking is probably the number one obstacle in your life that will hold you back and keep you stuck in the past. When you catch yourself wallowing in self-pity or engaging in the game of self-doubt, stop.

You may not believe this, but many celebrities suffer from insecurity and self-doubt. Yet they have trained themselves with strategies to deal with and respond to these emotions. If you are stuck in a toxic and negative interaction with somebody, it can be easier to try and escape the situation and not deal with what is happening. What you must do is stay with it; don't pretend it is not happening. It is important to face situations head-on, however negative, and refuse to give your power away to others. Remain calm, concentrated, aware, alert, and centered in the reality of the interaction until you can get away and un-clutter your mind from the onslaught. Try not to speak much, unless you absolutely have to. Simply listen, pay attention, and don't take the nearest escape route!

A Savvy Money Gal directs her thoughts to where she wants them to go.
I would like to encourage you towards redirecting your thoughts. When you are faced with a situation or person that for some reason makes you question yourself, pause and reflect as to why that is. Redirect your negative thoughts to something more positive. Treat yourself as you would a dog or a child: be kind and firm, and redirect yourself. This may feel funny when you do it for the first time, but keep trying and you will find you can redirect yourself time and time again. You may become very connected to your soul by practicing this strategy; it is very effective with animals, especially dogs. I practice redirecting my dogs all the time. Children can also benefit from redirection. 'In-the-moment self-coaching' is a phrase I like to use to identify redirection. This is when you catch yourself thinking or reacting to something negatively and redirecting yourself to something that will generate more positive outcomes.

> *"Out of clutter, find simplicity. From discord, find harmony.*
> *In the middle of difficulty lies opportunity."*
> **Albert Einstein (1879-1955) Theoretical Physicist**

Unclutter Your Mind

The mind is a very powerful tool in our lives. If your mind is wandering because it is full of clutter, it will impede you from practicing mindfulness; it will hold you back from moving forward in your life. By preventing cobwebs from being woven into your mind, it is possible to transform your existence in a way you probably never imagined. A key understanding must emerge from reading this chapter: it is imperative that women are mindful of the ongoing, daily challenges that will likely arise as they practice keeping their minds clear. It is not possible for women to let their guards down with respect to mindfulness.

You might be wondering what this has to do with managing money better. It has everything to do with managing money better. If your mind is cluttered, you are not free to pursue your goals and take charge of your life. You may be making mindless decisions with your money because you can't think clearly, and are most probably consumed by old stories that

Confidence Booster
Use the power of your mind to find financial freedom.

no longer suit who you are today and who you are becoming. Often we can't stop thinking about past money mistakes, and in doing so we become blocked in our ability to see or plan our financial future. Most of us carry baggage about money ill-spent. Our legacy from the past can be so all-consuming that it can paralyze us from moving forward and embracing newness or change. Sometimes, there are a lot of unresolved feelings, and letting go is just too daunting. Sometimes, holding on to the same old, same old is easier than forging a new path ahead.

Some of us may have experienced trying to make a decision about our money and found we are unable to do so. We take days and agonize about the right solution, but for some reason it never appears. We consult our friends, experts, and even the cashier at the grocery store as we search for an answer. It does not appear. We ultimately make a decision we are not overly comfortable with, but because of a deadline, we feel we have no choice. This is when buyer's remorse or money regrets come in to play. This holds particularly true when the outcome or result is not what we wanted.

There are effectively two types of clutter bombarding you on a daily basis. The first cluster of clutter sets up cobwebs in your head originating from your thoughts and emotional processes; the second cluster of clutter sets up cobwebs originating from your subconscious reactions to your physical environment, such as incidents and interactions with others that occur daily from your home, office, car, public transportation, or public places; basically any place where you interact with others. Despite its origin, all clutter moves through and is processed by your mind and will affect your daily choices surrounding how you spend your money. Unless mindfulness, self-awareness, and self-care are continually practiced, you may end up with problems of over-spending and unmanageable debt.

Managing Stress

A Savvy Money Gal manages the stressors in her life.

Ongoing awareness of the stressors in your life contributes to mindfulness as you manage your daily physical environments and mental processes. "Stress" is a term that is typically used to describe a by-product of emotions and thoughts as they are being processed through the mind. However the word "stress" is also used to describe physical and other stressors, that have nothing to do with processing emotions and thought processes. It is important that women learn to recognize and understand the source of their stress, so that those around them can also understand and be supportive. It is important to recognize that there are a myriad uses for the word "stress" and to be aware of how you, personally, use the word in your communication with others.

Stress may be a combination of thoughts, feelings, physical effects, and behaviours triggered in response to our perception that there is a threat to either our physical or emotional well-being.

Money worries create stress. Money worries may make women sick, by generating stress reactions that reduce their emotional well-being.

Mindful Meditation

Leading North American businesses have embraced mindfulness and meditation. They are seeing the benefits of greater productivity; their employees are becoming increasingly centered, calm and aware, and making better and more informed life and work balance choices. Target, Google, Twitter, Facebook, General Mills and Sun Life Financial are just some of the organizations that have embraced helping their employees to increase their ability to be mindful. Mindfulness training has also helped organizations retain employees who are best suited to their culture and values. In essence, mindfulness and meditation increases awareness, and through greater insight and choice they can transform who you are and how you engage in any activity.

The Buddha said that a person should establish mindfulness in one's day-to-day life maintaining, as much as possible, a calm awareness of one's body, feelings, and mind. Mindfulness, in one context, is an attentive awareness of the reality of things (especially of the present moment) and is an antidote to delusion about one's circumstances. Mindfulness becomes a power when it is in tandem with a clear comprehension of what is taking place. Mindfulness can be traced back to the earlier Upanishads, part of Hindu scripture.

Meditation refers to a state where your body and mind are consciously relaxed and focused. Practitioners of this art report increased awareness, focus and concentration, as well as a more positive outlook on life. Although there are many different approaches to meditation, the fundamental principles remain the same. The most important principles are those of removing obstructive, negative, and wandering thoughts, and calming the mind with a deep sense of focus. This clears the mind of debris and prepares it for a higher quality of activity.

Negative thoughts, as discussed previously, can benefit greatly from the practice of mindful meditation. Shutting these thoughts out allows for the cleansing of the mind, so that it may focus on deeper, more meaningful messages from the soul. Some practitioners even shut out all sensory input – no sights, no sounds, and nothing to touch – and try to detach themselves from the commotion around them. You may focus on a deep, profound thought if this is your goal. It may seem uncomfortable at first, since we are all too accustomed to constantly hearing and seeing things. However, as you continue this exercise, you will find yourself becoming more aware of everything around you.

A Savvy Money Gal controls her thoughts.
Our thoughts are very powerful. They affect our general attitude. Positive thoughts have a filling effect. They are admittedly invigorating. Positive people energize those around them. An article

in Psychology Today on the benefits of meditation stated that meditation has been shown to produce a wide range of mental benefits when practiced on a daily basis. Studies have shown that it can actually change how the brain processes information and how the brain manages the effects of stress, depression, and anxiety. Research has demonstrated that those who practice meditation are happier and calmer than their counterparts who don't. Meditation is not a new approach, it dates back centuries to Hindu and Buddhist philosophies. Recently, the University of Miami has developed a proven approach to help people become more mindful. The University believes that engaging in daily mindfulness workouts can increase your health and happiness. They promote a ten to fifteen minute mindfulness exercise designed to increase your focus, and to increase a broad awareness of sensations and surroundings. To learn more visit: www.miamimindfulness.org/index.html .

For some people, yoga has replaced mindful meditation as the best way to find relaxation and manage negative thoughts. Yoga helps to strengthen and increase the range of motion in your body. It promotes flexibility, stamina, and balance, ultimately leading to living in a more relaxed state with increased energy. Many women practicing yoga have seen the many benefits it can have on their lives.

Exercises

Exercise #1
Start taking time out each day to give thanks for all the good things you have in your life. There is no doubt you have much to be grateful for. When we approach each day with feelings of thanks, we are able to deal much better with life's stresses and challenges. Over the next thirty days, take sixty seconds in the morning and again at night to think about your blessings.

Exercise #2
Think about exploring yoga programs in your neighbourhood or close to work. Take a trial class. Talk to the instructors in terms of what you can expect, and the related benefits. Believe me when I say that yoga has the power and ability to help you get to a better place physically and mentally.

Connecting with You

1. How are you enjoying expressing your personal affirmation? Do you find it is helping you to achieve more success and get more focused on where you want to go in life?

_____

_____

2. How is your daily journal writing progressing? What surprised you in your entries?

_____

_____

3. Are you honoring your pledge to yourself to make sacred time weekly to focus on yourself and your top financial priorities? How are you enjoying Personal Finance Friday?

_____

_____

4. How did you feel about engaging in mindful meditation? Is it working for you? If so, explain. If not, what is holding you back from finding success with it?

_____

_____

5. What went well for you as you went through this chapter?

_____

_____

Chapter Two ~ Strategy #2
Stop Living in the Past and Look to the Future

"Clinging to the past is the problem. Embracing change is the solution."
Gloria Steinem (1934-) Feminist Activist

Personal Learning Goal

As you read through this chapter, you will learn to identify and define your money values; to determine where you are today, where you want to go, and what you need to get there. You will learn about how the past may be holding you back, and to recognize old values and ideas about money you may be carrying around with you. You will consider how living in the past is keeping you stuck. You will be acknowledging and accepting the past, letting it go, and finding inner peace.

This chapter builds on embracing a winning attitude. As you learn to manage self-doubt, you are preparing yourself for looking ahead to possibilities. Leaving your past money mistakes behind will push you ahead. When you strengthen your emotional well-being by giving yourself an emotional and mental boost, you will move away from living in the past and start afresh.

Making a fresh start with your money and leaving the past behind will give you energy, focus, and clarity about who you are and what matters to you. You are poised to make better choices for yourself, because you now have finally released old stories that no longer reflect who you are today. Your future will look brighter, and you will be more carefree and less connected to the past. You will no longer engage in pity and will acquire a new perspective on how you value and use your money. For example, you may learn to embrace your past for what it is and forge ahead with your future with newfound optimism and clarity, determined not to make the same mistakes again. You will learn not to beat yourself up about past mistakes and to set a new course. This is more than a money makeover; you actually leave your past mistakes behind, transform how you think, and make the future your focus.

When the past speaks, the present and future are silent. When we live in the past, we deny ourselves growth opportunities, restrict our future growth, and obstruct our unrealized life dreams and goals.

A Savvy Money Gal learns from the past but looks to the future.

Each and every one of us has a past. Haven't we all made mistakes with our money at some point? Past mistakes can keep us stuck holding on to perceptions and attitudes that are outdated, and that neither reflect the person we are today, nor what we value. In order to practice mindfulness, self-awareness, and self-care, women are required to live in the moment and take one day at a time.

Money Story: Sharon

Years ago, Sharon mortgaged the entire value of her home to pay for a new business opportunity that she thought was destined to be a success. She parted with her money because her only daughter was in need of additional funds to fulfill her dream. What mother wouldn't give money to her children in order for them to fulfill their dreams?

Unfortunately, the recession hit in the 1990s and money that was supposed to be made, never materialized. When the bank started calling for loan payments, there was no additional money to pay the installments. In fact, Sharon and her family were broke. They had invested all of the equity in their home into this new business venture, thinking it would be successful. Not only did Sharon lose her family home but for the next twenty-five years she lived with regret, sorrow, and sadness about her financial decisions that led to the loss. Sharon did not consult with a financial expert. She had not anticipated the recession that hit, no one could have. Sharon now lives in poverty on a very modest government pension with little money for extras. Her retirement is on a shoe string budget. She has learned to forgive herself and to count the blessings she has each and every day. She has come to terms with the fact that the decision her family made was ill-informed and high risk. The other upside to this situation is she has taught her children the value of getting expert advice and never to put the family home at risk.

Sharon's story is a tragic one, but it reminds us of how past money mistakes can have a lifetime effect. Making intelligent and savvy financial choices that are grounded in mindfulness, self-awareness, and self-care are important. It is always wise to consult financial experts before making any major financial decisions.

We can all relate to Sharon's story; it serves to remind us how human we are and demonstrates how women may do anything for their children. We often will sacrifice our financial future for them. Sharon's story could have been different. There are many alternative financial choices she could have made, if she had recognized the value of seeking financial advice. She will likely live out her lifetime with the economic consequences of one major ill-informed financial decision. Many women think they need to manage their money on their own and make their own decisions. While this is true, we must be empowered before making financial decisions, they must be informed decisions. Sharon was not informed. As an aside, no one should ever mortgage their home and use the money to pursue any type of business. The risk is too high.

If you want to achieve more and feel in control of your life, setting personal goals is essential. When you stop living out old money habits or patterns and redirect your money towards your goals, you will achieve them. It doesn't matter how much money you have or make, or whether you are just starting out or have a successful career, by opening yourself up to new possibilities through goal setting, you will start living the life you want. You must also evaluate how you live your life daily. This is different from living day to day. It is more about being present in your life and conscious of your daily choices.

Confidence Booster
When major financial decisions must be made, seek expert advice and explore your options.

How to Leave Your Money Past Behind

> *"Hope is a walking dream."*
> **Aristotle (384-322 BC) Philosopher**

A Savvy Money Gal has a past, but has left it behind.
None of us want to be reminded of past mistakes or failed attempts. Whether they are failed relationships, jobs, friendships or money mistakes, they hurt. The pain can stay for a very long time. Every one of us has done things in our past that we regret. If we were born with the knowledge we require to avoid mistakes throughout our lives, we probably wouldn't make most of our mistakes; but this is not reality.

In order to leave the past behind, you need to make a conscious choice to live in the present. Our past mistakes are a reminder to us not to keep repeating a pattern. We must be mindful of the past and the triggers that have created problems for us. You never really leave your past behind (it's there) but you learn to make better choices for yourself resulting in better outcomes.

Many of us live in deep emotional pain from the past. It is hard for me to say that I can understand all the problems other women face, because I can't. What I can say is by raising your consciousness about your past money habits, and acknowledging the pain or mistakes of your past, you can forge a new future for yourself. Old money habits die hard. By getting really present with yourself – your mind and your emotions— it is amazing how easy it can be to set yourself free. It's your choice.

A Savvy Money Gal learns from her mistakes. They don't define her.
Money mistakes are like failed relationships. We move on, but we never really let go. Men are excellent at letting go of the past and moving forward. Money mistakes or problems don't seem

to define men for as long as they do for women. All of us have felt the emotional pain of bad money decisions. The pain goes away, but the thoughts, feelings, and emotions tend to stay for a very long time, continually rising up from our subconscious to try and enter our mind again.

I tell many women that if they really want to leave their money past behind, they have to really want to change. Motivation is key. Motivation can come from your own personal desire or from an external source – like your husband, children, or friends. Think hard about what truly motivates you.

Confidence Booster
Life events can change everything. Don't wait for something bad to happen before you take control of your financial future.

Money Story: June

June no longer lives in the past, although she spent years wallowing in self-pity and not moving forward. Her life and money were formerly cluttered. Prior to her divorce, June's husband managed the family finances, so she basically stepped away from her responsibilities to manage her money. And, she had a sizeable monthly allowance of money given to her by her husband for household expenses. She didn't have to account for how she spent the money, because her husband did not really care, as long as the home was looked after and dinner was on the table. Over a period of time, June acquired an unhealthy disrespect for money. She really didn't care much about it, because it didn't mean anything to her. She felt that the money was never really "hers", and didn't value her contribution to the family. She used the money she received to manage the household, but she didn't value it.

After her divorce, June struggled with managing her money and made countless errors. Each time she attempted to get a handle on her situation and started learning about personal finance, she found reasons to abandon the plan. Lack of time was the excuse she used. Her unhealthy lack of respect for money began to sabotage her in ways she never imagined. She didn't open her bills. Then when her mother died everything came crashing down. Becoming the Executor of her mother's will forced her to engage with money more. She really had no choice. As an only child she was it. Her mother left her entire estate to June.

> *"We are not perfect, but we are stronger and wiser than the sum of our errors."*
> **Audre Lorde (1934-1992) Writer and Activist**

June sought coaching. I worked with her to help her understand why and how she had acquired such disrespect for money. We spent time learning about her money values and the reasons behind the choices June made. This took time to resolve, but unearthing her values and perceptions helped her to understand some of her self-sabotaging behaviours. Self-sabotage manifested in many ways, but was primarily rooted in her lack of confidence. The conditions were never created to help her grow. What we found was that she was intimidated by money and wealth. Her husband had kept tight control of the money and allocated it to her as if she were a child. Her diminished self-confidence was the result of her lifelong mismanagement of money and was one of the effects she took away from a bad marriage.

We spent time rebuilding June's self-confidence and self-worth. It took time. As June began to rebuild herself, she started down a new money path. Yet, she was embarrassed by her lack of sophistication or her lack of money savvy. June felt ashamed that, at the age of thirty-eight, she was more like a dependent child than a fully functioning woman. These negative thoughts about herself contributed to her feeling of powerlessness, and we had to work hard to eradicate this problem.

We came up with a range of coping strategies that would help June diminish and manage the negativity in her mind. We also worked through her conflicting thoughts, emotions, and feelings that arose as a result of being married to a very successful businessman. On the one hand, part of the marriage was wonderful. Yet, parts of it left her feeling lost. Her marriage was often a contradiction.

June's journey to become more financially independent was triggered by two major life-altering events: the breakdown of her marriage and the death of her mother. It was through these defining events that she was forced to change for the better. Many of June's insecurities surfaced during her marriage. June told me that she was inherently insecure and that marrying a successful businessman had made her feel more secure. We learned, however, that more than economic helplessness had resulted from her marriage. June had also become emotionally helpless, and had to learn to stand in her own strength.

For many women, a life event will trigger a change in behaviour. June has now become more at peace with herself and her money. She sought out an investment advisor to invest her inheritance. A sudden increase in wealth can often result in a person squandering the money if they don't have good money strategies. Luckily, June set up a monthly spending plan and budget to track where her money goes. She has set several goals for herself and has mapped out timelines and the financial resources she needs to achieve them. She is slowly learning about investing and managing her own money.

In summary, June is doubting herself less and increasing her self-confidence. As she continues to embrace her life as a single woman, she is more optimistic about her future. With the help of a circle of expert financial advisors to provide professional guidance, she is rebuilding herself into a much stronger woman. She is managing her negative thoughts and making positive affirmations and visualizations. She is learning to expand her mind and to recognize the possibilities that emerge. She is no longer boxed in, but navigating her life with clarity, confidence, and control.

What are Your Life and Money Priorities?

A Savvy Money Gal defines her life priorities.

Before we go any further, now might be a good time to think about where you are in your life and where you want to go. Consider where you are today with your financial and life priorities. Remember, your future financial success always starts from today. At each stage of your life, there are distinct events or rites of passage that are not necessarily related to your age. For instance, you might be having a child in your forties in a second marriage, rather than in your twenties. There are no predefined parameters of what needs to happen at a certain age. Age matters in the sense that it is a guide post only, so do not get hung up on how old you are.

> 20s, 30s, 40s, 50s, 60s, and 70+
> Pioneering, Growing, Settling, Retiring

Pioneering

Preparing for your future and getting more education are essential. As you start out, you will probably be getting your first real job (not that your summer jobs were not real); paying off school debts; starting to or trying to save more money; and spending most of your time and spare money on entertainment, such as going out with your friends and enjoying some truly memorable life experiences. These are your optimistic years when everything seems possible and the world is your oyster. Taking the time to plan your life and to set goals is essential for getting on the road to financial success.

Growing

You are finally on your way. These are the years of FIRSTS -- first home, first committed relationship, first child, and first promotion. You will be feeling a sense of accomplishment now and will be cautiously optimistic about your future. Family and career demands will be front and centre for you. You will start to venture into uncharted territory and might be feeling a little uneasy with all the changes in your life. Getting the most out of your life matters and doing something you enjoy is essential.

Establishing and Settling

You are starting to feel established. At this phase, you will be growing your assets and starting to see a small nest egg or cushion growing. You will be paying down your mortgage, saving more for your retirement years (60+), and continuing to save for your children's education or starting to help them with their post-secondary education. These are the years when everything comes together. Preparing for the unexpected should be on your radar by getting life and disability insurance, as well as ensuring you have an up-to-date will.

Retiring

Retirement may be a very long period of your life, perhaps twenty to thirty years. At this time, most women are paying off debt and creating a plan for their future. Many may be living alone. You will want to be prepared to make some lifestyle changes to accommodate your needs. You may be planning to fulfill some long-held dreams. You will also be thinking about such things as your estate and creating a personal legacy. In addition, you finally have time to give back to the community. These years are about creating joy, meaning, and purpose in your life. At the same time, you want to be carefully monitoring your spending and any health issues. It is important to ensure that you have enough money to last you to age one hundred. Prosperity of the soul becomes a driving force during the rekindling years.

Where Are You Today?

Recognize what life stage you are currently at. It matters. Each phase offers growth, newness, and some element of change. The more you are aware of the challenges each phase provides, the better you can prepare for what lies ahead. As much as you would like to orchestrate everything in your life, life doesn't always happen that way. Life stages provide us with indications as to priorities and financial considerations, though they are not carved in stone.

Navigating Changes in Your Life

Most women today have gone through at least one, if not several, major life transitions. Such events have the power to change everything. Major transitions include divorce, the death of a close family member or spouse, or job loss or job elimination. When these types of transitions happen, they can be heart breaking and painful. It's a time of evaluation, when we reflect on our lives, where we've been and where we're headed. Then there are minor transitions, such as a promotion at work, or a child graduating from school. While these transitions don't rock your world, they do cause you to think about your priorities.

In total, there are about nine life events of major importance. Most of them are ones you can plan for, but some could be unforeseen. Some of the planned events will probably be part of the Big Picture goals that are part of your life. We will be spending time later in this book creating them or refining goals you already have. So let's review our list and see if you agree...

Nine Major Life Transitions or Events

A Savvy Money Gal takes control over her life.

How women respond to a life event or big change is essential to their health. Feeling good about your life and your money at all times matters. When faced with an unexpected event or crisis, you need to take stock of your life. Remember it does not matter where you are or how much money you have, the journey to getting back on track is the same.

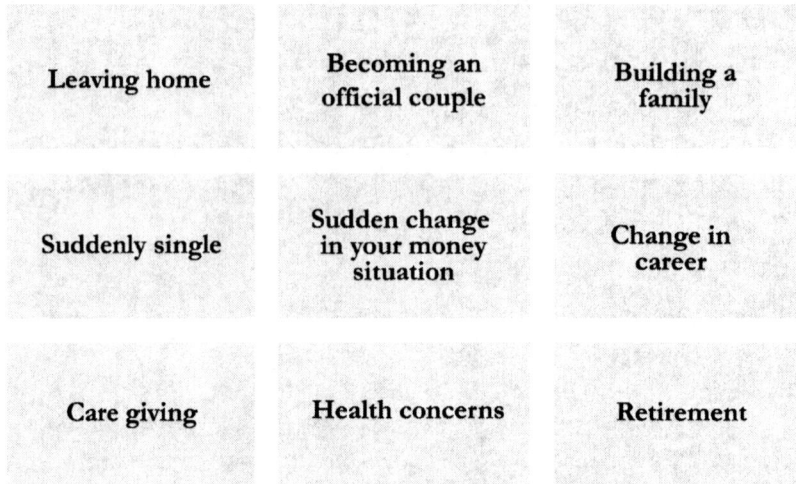

Leaving home	**Becoming an official couple**	**Building a family**
Suddenly single	**Sudden change in your money situation**	**Change in career**
Care giving	**Health concerns**	**Retirement**

There is so much of life that we don't control. There are particular times when a life event occurs that is incredibly profound. Some people call these "moments of truth". I characterize a moment of truth as a defining moment. When they occur, they shake our foundation. For example, the loss of a spouse or parent is a defining moment because there are lifelong implications resulting from this loss. These defining moments are tough to get over.

A defining moment puts your life in motion. Life transitions can be divided into two broad categories: planned and unexpected. Planned life transitions are ones that you can easily work with, they are usually already on your radar. Typically, although not always, planned events tend to be the happier events in our lives because we map them out. It is the unexpected events that can cause us havoc because we are often unprepared.

An unexpected event can change everything. Each of us responds differently to change in our lives. A transition or life event is a time of change and you need to have a strategy in place for dealing with such a change. An essential step may be to build a circle or group of Go To people who can help you manage through such changes. Surround yourself with people who believe in your dreams. The life transition may result in a loss or gain for you. Losses are the most difficult to work through. Gains can also be challenging. Still, we want you to have hope. You will come through these events if you control your life by taking specific steps to get yourself back on track. Make no mistake; a life transition or event can take you temporarily off your path.

Are there any BIG changes going on in your LIFE right now? If so, what are they?

_____

_____

Get Back on Track Today

Pause and reflect on the life event. It is easy to get into problem-solving and action mode, but the most essential thing for you to do first is to take a step back and assess what is happening.

> *"Difficult times have helped me to understand better than before how infinitely rich and beautiful life is in every way, and that so many things that one goes worrying about are of no importance whatsoever."*
> **Karen Blixen (1885-1962) Danish Writer and Autobiographer**

Pause. Reflect. Nurture yourself. It is not wise to rush into any decisions or actions. You need to really understand what is going on and the implications to you and your life.

Own your feelings. This is where the work really begins. It is easy to dismiss or bury how you are feeling and just move on. This is a fairly common coping skill. However, any buried feelings will resurface sometime later in your life. Any life events and their associated feelings and emotions that you do not resolve will have major impacts on your future relationships and your money.

Assess how this event may impact your Big Picture and your saving or spending goals. Everyone has a Big Picture and if you don't, you don't need to worry; we will help you create one. Now would be a good time to do some self-analysis, but don't spend too much time on it.

Reach out to an expert for help. By the term "expert", I mean someone who specializes in an area of interest. For example, if you find yourself suddenly single or widowed, it is essential you speak to a family lawyer or a divorce lawyer, and even engage a will and estate lawyer. Although it is assumed most women have the ability to be savvy, unless you are an expert, get advice. Don't try to figure things out on your own because you may not have the in-depth knowledge and understanding of laws, the banking system etc., to help you work through your life transition. Also, the life transition may have a big impact on your Big Picture Goals and dreams, and quite possibly may have an unforeseen money expense.

Review your life in a couple of months. Make sure you update or change relevant documents, such as your disability insurance, financial plan, and will and estate plan. When a life event occurs there are major impacts, so you need to be prepared.

Working through a life event will take time and some personal self-reflection. Working through a life transition as it happens is important and you have to allow yourself enough time to get settled. If by chance you are not going through any life events at this point in your life, you may find yourself needing to come back to this section when one arises. As well as un-cluttering our minds, we also need to un-clutter our lives when we have an immediate and burning issue arising as a life event. Otherwise, you may be stalled from moving forward on your journey in this program.

Your Money Values

A Savvy Money Gal lives a value-based life.
What we think is reflected by how we behave. Learning about your money perceptions and values will help you to get to know yourself better and provide insight on the decisions you make about your money. Often we are unaware of why we do some of the things we do. We engage in mindless spending or unconscious spending, but don't know why. We will go through some exercises to help you understand your money past. As we move forward and start to unearth your money values, each of you will have a different starting point or point of reference. This reference point matters, because it is the lens through which you will peer backward and review your lifelong money values and habits. Once you understand exactly where you are today, it will be much easier to map out a pathway for moving forward on the road to financial success.

A Savvy Money Gal is curious about the world.
In your quest to improve your life and live more comfortably, it is essential that you seek knowledge and receive answers to your money questions. With enhanced clarity about your money you will make more informed financial decisions. Often we make decisions with imperfect or limited information, but some information is better than no information. Personal insight or self-awareness is also imperative to successful money management. The more you know about your values or value system, including your money values, the more capable you will be as you steer yourself in directions you never thought possible.

Our money values are similar to other personal values, such as truth, honesty, or fairness. They reflect your behaviour and the choices you make for yourself. You don't consciously think about your values, because they are so deeply rooted in who you are, but they guide your decisions every day. However, what if you are living in the present with old money values that do not reflect who you are today and where you are going? The importance of knowing your money values will help you to understand better how you view and manage your money.

The decisions we make are often grounded in our money values. For example, when we are in our twenties and have little responsibility in our lives, many of us spend our money on entertainment. But, as we mature and grow older our value system changes, particularly when we marry and have children. As we grow older and transition to our retirement years, we may spend more time focused on creating a personal legacy for ourselves and our families. Our values shift. We may give more of ourselves. Our values may lead us to concentrate less on making money, and focus more on preserving what we have in terms of leaving a legacy for our children, grandchildren or other individuals who matter to us. In addition, a desire to leave a lasting, personal legacy may include participating in social causes, activism, community work, volunteering, teaching, and a myriad of other contributions to society.

Our Childhood Money Lessons

Most of us learned a money lesson or two when we were kids. For some of us our introduction into the use of money, our childhood money lessons, might have been very uneventful. For others, the process might have been rather bumpy. My childhood money story describes how I learned to stand in my own strength and become financial independent at a very young age. How about you?

Most of us did not receive specific money management training from our parents. Perhaps your parents had less-than-stellar skills to pass on, because they did not learn money management skills in their childhoods. Around the age of seven, research indicates that children really begin to grasp what money is and its value. Up until then, money is an abstract concept for most children; they are too young to really comprehend and understand its value. Our parents or guardians may have rarely talked about money, so most of our monetary learning and understanding came from the school yard and our perceptions shaped by television and other media. This is not a rich education by any means.

Confidence Booster
Start today by teaching your children good money values. Engage them daily in your money management activities.

Money Story: Jackie

Jackie was born in 1954, a Canadian boomer born midway between 1946 and 1962. While growing up, her family had only two channels on their television. She can't remember ever watching television much at all as a child, especially not money-related programming. Sunday nights were the exception, when she watched the Ed Sullivan Show and Bonanza. Being working class, her parents impressed upon her and her siblings the need to work hard for money. In her neighbourhood, most children around the ages of eight or nine started working at odd jobs, like most of her friends did. She remembers receiving a small allowance as a child, as did most of her friends, but it was minimal, enough to buy one coke and a packet of chips per week. Any other money she had to earn herself. She had to beg her mother for money to get into the movies on Saturdays if she had not found an odd job. This taught her and her generation the value of money in their childhood and teenage years.

Jackie believes this training is much less defined in children of the boomer generation, known as Generation X, who are now the ones busy raising families and working at the same time. During Jackie's childhood, most mothers stayed at home. This meant there was little money, but lots of training about how to obtain it by working. In her case, her parents always talked about money, and so did the parents of most of her friends. She believes that when you don't have a lot of money, you talk about it a lot.

There are many generational differences today between how Boomers, Generation X, and Millennials manage their money. Boomers are generally defined as being born between 1946-1964, Generation X between 1965-1979 and Generation Y, also known as the Millennials, between 1980-2000. Where do you see yourself? Are you a Boomer, Generation X or Millennial?

Many people today believe that money values should be learned at school, but I strongly believe that money values should be taught by children's best teachers – their parents. Our money values shape what we believe, what we think and how we behave with money. Money lessons are life-long lessons that can't be learned in front of a computer or at school; they are better learned at home, from parents and family. Schools can play a wonderful role in teaching the investing terms, but how you manage your money really comes from your values, and values are learned at home. Some believe that a little deprivation in childhood, instead of indulgence, may be the right approach to teaching money management skills early. What do you think? In the end, it is through practical application, trial and error, that we learn about money and the value of it.

Having good financial intelligence is not about saving tons of money or investing it well. It is about developing a healthy understanding of your relationship with money. With clarity and greater understanding, you will increase your confidence. It's that simple! With increased confidence comes better decisions and conversations about your money, ultimately leading to a sense of control and mastery over your destiny.

Money Journeys

There have been times in my life when I was concerned about my financial future, embarrassed by my past money mistakes and worried that I couldn't get ahead. Regret and remorse have been in my money vocabulary. This never stopped me though from pursuing my goals and dreams. My solid family values supported my steadfast strength to reach my goals, and guided me to where I am today. My Money Story starts at the age of eight or nine when I began to understand the power of money as a tool to get to where I wanted to go to in life. This inspired me to start a series of successful entrepreneurial endeavours that ultimately led me to where I am today.

> *"It is the function of art to renew our perception. What we are familiar with we cease to see. The writer shakes up the familiar scene, and, as if by magic, we see a new meaning in it."*
> **Anais Nin (1903-1977) French Writer and Diarist**

My Money Story is one of insight and understanding at an early age. What I learned at a very early age was to stand in my own strength, much like my Mother did. In Chapter Five, I share with you more anecdotes and passages from my story, but suffice it to say that my money journey was guided by my passion and interests in life.

Mother Teresa started her life with no money at all. But through her life journey and humanitarian efforts to relieve suffering, she raised lots of money for her charity work. Mother Teresa ran organizations that helped people with HIV/AIDS, leprosy, and tuberculosis. She lived her life doing what she loved and in the end made money for her cause. She received countless awards for her sainthood. Her pursuit was not to make money; it was to help mankind. This was Mother Teresa's money story.

Warren Buffett expressed interest in making and saving money early in his life. He started making money very young by selling chewing gum door-to-door. While in high school, he made money by delivering newspapers, and selling golf balls and stamps. The early encouragement he received set him on his money journey towards success as a CEO. This was Warren Buffett's money story.

The 'Reference Point' at the Root of Your Money Values

Below is an exercise that contains a series of thought provoking questions designed to reveal your "reference point", the place where all your money values originated from. This "reference point" is the lens through which you will peer backward and review your lifelong money values. Answer these questions as we continue along our journey of self-discovery to unearth your money values. Consider these questions in the context of your life and who you are today.

Remember that there are no right or wrong answers. Each of us has a unique money story to tell. For some of you, your history will be uneventful. For others, you may have had many defining moments.

Exercises

Your Money Roots

1. Where do you come from? What are your family roots? Are you a small town gal or a big city gal?

_____

_____

2. What recollections of money do you have from childhood?

_____

_____

3. Looking back at your life, how would you say that money or the lack of money is impacting your life today?

_____

_____

4. Did you experience any BIG changes or life events that defined money for you?

_____

_____

Your Money Experiences

5. What messages have you received about money that you think have shaped your attitude toward money? Have you experienced discrimination or prejudice around your money? What negative imagery do you see around women and money that you don't like?

_____

_____

_____

6. What life changes have you experienced? For example, the loss of a business or becoming the breadwinner? How have these impacted you?

_____

_____

_____

Your Money Feelings

7. Do you have regrets about your money? What would they be?

_____

_____

_____

8. What one big money mistake do you carry with you today that you can't release? Why have you been unable to let it go?

_____

_____

9. In your opinion, what could you do to let this go and move forward?

_____

_____

_____

10. Do you think money or the lack of money is holding you back from getting the life you want? Why? Why not?

_____

_____

_____

Seeds of Change

11. What one bad money habit do you have that you wish to overcome? Who could help you?

_____

_____

_____

12. What are your money values today? (Use any words to describe them.)

_____

_____

_____

Connecting with You

1. Are you honoring your pledge to yourself to put aside sacred time to focus on your top priorities? If you invest the time, you will get what you need out of this book and get to where you need to go on your financial journey. Remember, you can go through this book at your own pace.

_____

_____

2. How is your journal writing progressing? What is surprising you about your entries?

_____

_____

3. What were your experiences going through the money values exercise in this chapter? What one thing are you going to take away from this exercise?

_____

_____

4. Often many of us feel we don't have enough money in our life to reach our goals or live more comfortably. Do you feel this way and if so, why?

_____

_____

Chapter Three ~ Strategy #3
Be Authentic: Live Within your Means

"If only we would stop trying to be happy, we'd have a pretty good time."
Edith Wharton (1862-1937) American Writer

Personal Learning Goal

Through this chapter you will begin to understand the power of being authentic. Today, people are craving authenticity from others. Getting real with ourselves is also closely tied to getting real with our money: using our money in authentic and value-based ways. You will have to consider whether you are a saver, spender, or somewhere in between, and how your mood can impact what you do with your money. You will shift from spending money on things you don't really need and toward thinking about your money in the context of your future. You will engage in conscious choices, watch what you do with your money, and make mindful money decisions. You will continue to develop strategies that will assist you to get very real with your life and your money.

This chapter builds on the first two where we spent time showing you the importance of having a winning money mindset and that through positive affirmation and visualization you can create mental images for where you want to be. We also discussed the importance of leaving the past behind and looking to the future. These powerful strategies will empower you to move forward and embrace what's ahead, instead of holding on to attitudes, feelings, and thoughts about your money that you have outgrown.

False or Unauthentic Money

False money involves the notion of creating a lifestyle for yourself that is pretentious. It is money that is used to increase status and impress people you don't necessarily like. When you engage in using money to impress others, you are essentially engaging in "money bullying." False money may be connected to either spending with borrowed money, money on credit, or spending money you already have. In most instances, people use borrowed money to create a façade and subsidize a "living large" lifestyle in their quest to increase their circle of friends and their status.

False money is the great pretender that differentiates between need and want. False money allows you to buy what you want, rather than what you need. It sets you up to spend money mindlessly. False money could manifest in having very large balances on your credit card or having a super-sized mortgage for a big house you can't really afford. False money is spent to get people to like you and to elevate your status. This money isn't real; it takes on a false identity. Sometimes false money can be used in an attempt to "keep up" with our neighbours or friends. This is referred to as "keeping up with the Joneses."

What is "Keeping up with the Joneses"?

The term "keeping up with the Joneses" is 20th century American. It originated with Arthur (Pop) Momand's Keep Up With The Joneses comic strip in the New York Globe. The strip was first published in 1913 and became popular quite quickly. By September 1915, a cartoon film of the same name was routing US cinemas. The 'Joneses' in the cartoon weren't based on anyone in particular, and they weren't portrayed in the cartoon itself. Jones was a very common name and 'the Joneses' was merely a generic name for 'the neighbours'. The notion of keeping up with your neighbors through the acquisition of material items or things dates back a century.

Authentic Money

A Savvy Money Gal is authentic.

Authentic money is tangible, thoughtful, directed, and has a long-term vision. Moving from false money toward real money will transform how you earn, spend, save, and gift your money. Money that you hold yourself accountable for is money that is directed; you are no longer putting your head in the sand like an ostrich. When you are authentic with your money, you no longer have anything to prove to anyone. You are making conscious and mindful money choices. You are very present with your money and much more self-aware. You think twice before buying anything, you no longer engage in impulse buying, and you have nothing to regret. You live within your means and are conscious of all your money choices and decisions.

Becoming more authentic boosts emotional well-being. Your wonderful gifts and talents will shine and you will stop pretending to be someone you are not. You will start reviewing your life on a daily basis, in a mindful manner, to ensure you are living an authentic life.

My strategy is twofold. First, I will continue to help you work on mindful spending habits and to transform how you earn, spend, save, and give gifts of your money. Second, I will assist you to look at your future and how you want your life to unfold. I want you to learn how to abandon short-term thinking and embrace a long-term approach to your life. This means living well daily, while keeping your eye on your future.

For those who have been living a lie for a long time, isn't it about time to stop living with false money? I guarantee that once you do that you will sleep better at night, worry less about your money, and you'll start to feel better about yourself. I also want to give you a big hug for sticking with this and for really taking your life and your money seriously. Now might be a good time for a group hug. Take yourself seriously. If you feel anger, face it without flinching or hiding, and work through it; anger may be a very normal part of the process. You must practice self-care and be kind to yourself; you are letting go and redefining your former self, by becoming a new and improved version of yourself. Whatever emotions rise up as you work through your changes, they are a valuable part of your process and should never be ignored.

There are many examples of spending money in an authentic way. You can live within your means, spend wisely, and be conscious of your choices. You can make trade-offs. You can be aware that if you buy a pair of shoes for $100, you are making a conscious choice to do so, knowing that you will have a $100 delay in pursuing and reaching your goals. You can begin to shift your mindset away from conspicuous consumption to mindful and mental accounting of how you spend your money. You can begin to feel much more solid and grounded. You can make a spending plan and budget, and direct your extra money toward your future goals. You can pause when you shop and think twice before you spend. You can learn to know the difference between need and want. You can recognize that managing your money goes far beyond making a decision at the point of sale. You can train your mind to be conscious and aware of your financial choices.

A Savvy Money Gal is purposeful.

When we are authentic, we are purposeful in everything in our lives. Our money is directed toward planned goals and long-term financial security. "Whole money" is money that is used in a principled and reasonable way. We should spend it with an acceptance of who we are and use it with an understanding that we don't need to use our money to take away pain or feelings of unhappiness. When you love who you are, you feel whole. You are optimistic about your future and good enough is enough. You no longer try to be perfect. You are conscious about how you spend your money and aware that buying things won't make you happy. You no longer engage in impulse buying and compulsive shopping. If you are a consistent "feel good money spender" and find it hard to become a "whole money spender," you may want to consider working with trained professionals to get you out of this rut.

When we mend our broken hearts and manage our emotions, previous "feel good money spending" turns into "whole money spending". We feel more complete and whole within ourselves. Our need to self-medicate with money vanishes and in place come healthy attitudes and a relationship with our money that breaks dependency. Money becomes a partner and a trusted friend to help you live.

Financial Security - A State of Happiness, Energy, and Power

Financial security is the happiness, energy, and power we feel when our money is working for us in a way we deliberately want it to. This is deliberate and the result of conscious choices. As we embrace a winning mindset, leave the past behind, and start to live more authentically, we empower ourselves. These choices contribute to our feelings of "financial security" because we feel happy, energetic, and powerful. Remember...

Happiness + Energy + Power = Financial Security

Women frequently tell me their number one problem is a shortage of money. Yet, they have good jobs, live in nice homes, some have partners, creating dual income sharing, and many take nice vacations. I find it easy to understand why women on fixed, lower incomes tell me this. But why do eight out of ten women tell me this, even those with seemingly comfortable lifestyles? It is a mindset which reflects a false belief that the answer to money worries is more money. It also reflects a bad habit of not knowing where money is going.

Confidence Booster
Improve your relationship with your money and soon you will feel you have enough money to live comfortably.

The enormous hardship that women living on lower incomes endure is undeniable. For women who live in poverty, deprivation is their reality and it is a daily struggle to keep their heads above water. I do not want to minimize the ongoing struggles that poverty generates for women living on lower incomes. Yet, why are ninety nine percent of all women I know complaining about a shortage of money?

> *"To have that sense of one's intrinsic worth, which constitutes self-respect, is potentially to have everything: the ability to discriminate, to love, and to remain indifferent. To lack it is to be locked within oneself, paradoxically, incapable of either love or indifference."*
> **Joan Didion (1934-) Writer**

A Savvy Money Gal feels good about the money she has.

I have discovered through my business, that provides financial consulting services to women, that the feeling of abundance is not about how much income a woman has coming in on a monthly or yearly basis. Rather, it is totally related to their money values. How they feel about themselves, how they manage their mind and their emotions are directly connected to how they use, manage, save, and spend their money. How women use their money determines how much happiness, energy, and power they are experiencing. This is their level of financial security. It is directly related to the relationship a woman has with her soul. I find that ninety nine percent of women I encounter do not have a soulful relationship with their money. This is a major finding.

It is generally agreed that working women have less money to manage overall than working men do. We have the facts to back up our understanding of the male-to-female income difference. Yet, when partnerships form and two people combine their incomes, the consolidation may create a general money pool that minimizes the difference. Ultimately, it appears that optimizing whatever money is available to women can provide the core solution to the issue of not having a soulful relationship with their money. This core issue arises regardless of whether a woman is single and on a fixed, low income; single and working; in a partnership living on a fixed, low income; or in a partnership and working.

Current Research on the Relationship between Income and Happiness

Interestingly, if you think making a lot of money is the ticket to your happiness, you may be mistaken because research reveals this may not be the case. Research by experts Dr. Angus Deaton and Dr. Daniel Kahneman informs us that happiness quotients level off at around an annual income of $75,000. Beyond that, there does not appear to be an increase in overall happiness. As an individual or a family unit, you might be living on $300,000 annually; however, according to the research, there would be no greater increase in happiness than if $75,000 were the yearly income. Thus, maximum happiness peaks at $75,000.

To provide an opposite point of view, I refer to a May 2013 research paper published in the American Economic Review, written by economists Betsey Stevenson and Justin Wolfers from the University of Michigan. It disagrees with the findings of Deaton and Kahneman about what they called the 'satiation point', the optimal happiness level of individuals or families being at $75,000 a year. Stevenson and Wolfers concluded that satiation is roughly a straight line that does not diminish or increase as incomes rise. The overarching finding by these University of Michigan researchers- validated in both rich and poor countries— is that money does buy happiness, and that more money leads to more happiness! In fact, these researchers write "we find no evidence of a significant break in either the happiness-income relationship, nor in the life satisfaction-income relationship, even as annual incomes go up to half a million dollars."

As the above examples demonstrate, current research findings vary tremendously. I introduce them, not to get you hung up on the research, but to share what current literature is indicating about the relationship between income and happiness levels. There are no definitive answers. So, the question remains, can money buy you happiness?

Can Money Buy Your Happiness?

A Savvy Money Gal finds joy and meaning in her life, and defines what makes her happy.

If you are barely making ends meet, you may not be happy at all, especially if your paycheques are unreliable, inconsistent, and not meeting your current living expenses. This is understandable. The reality is that if you are making a lot of money, you have more choices and options, greater flexibility and empowerment. Higher income allows someone to concentrate on fulfilling their life goals, dreams, and passions. However, to do so, a higher-income person will have to practise the Savvy Money Gal Strategies.

Famous psychologist, Abraham Maslow, author of Motivation and Personality, created a hierarchy of human needs that refers to the process of fulfilling life goals, dreams, and passions. Someone with a lower income may be focused on meeting basic needs, such as food, shelter, and transportation— and this daily grind may drain all their energy and prevent them from reaching self-actualization. Some people who live on a low, fixed income may be generally happy. They may have found a way to live within their means; all their basic needs may be met; and their source of income, although low, may be very reliable. The biggest problem for this low-income category, however, is finding money for extras, such as extended health care, and dental costs.

Confidence Booster
Good money strategies are key to people of all income levels obtaining a state of financial security.

Yet, people who live on a higher income may not be living within their means, and even though their basic needs are being met, they may be spending their money lifelessly and not utilizing soulful money practices. A person on a higher income can get caught up in living beyond their means due to their ability to obtain credit. Thus, we can see that it doesn't really matter how much money is coming in, if it is not managed with our 6 Savvy Money Gal Strategies, there are going to be problems. Perhaps money can buy happiness if you practice good money strategies each and every day.

Perceptions of Money Relating to Happiness Levels

I want to share with you the interesting research of The Gallup-Healthways Well-Being Index® (www.well-beingindex.com), which studied a group of US residents over a period of time up to 2012. The study also collected feedback from over 450,000 people around the world regarding their perceptions of money and happiness. What they found is there are two ways to look at money and happiness: whether more money increases people's emotional well-being, and whether more money increases people's evaluation of their life.

A key finding is that people who have a high income tend to have higher "life satisfaction." Someone who has a low income is less likely to be happy, may have low life satisfaction and low emotional well-being. These research findings tell us that people with lower incomes are at a disadvantage and therefore money does play an important role in affecting life satisfaction, happiness, and emotional well-being.

Another key finding is that feeling good about yourself increases your emotional well-being. Negativity makes you feel horrible, and decreases your emotional well-being. A negative mood is most likely to trigger spending or to be an antecedent to spending. Feeling good about your life and your money will enhance how you feel. If you feel good about yourself and you embrace a winning money mindset about your money, the greater is the likelihood of feeling successful. Money has the power to make us happy, increase our emotional well-being, and life satisfaction.

Are you a Spender or Saver?

A Savvy Money Gal spends and saves her money wisely.

Which are you? A saver or a spender? According to Rick Scott, Cynthia Cryder and George Loewenstein, in their article on Tightwads and Spendthrifts, there are two types of money personalities. You are either a "spendthrift" or a "tightwad." A spendthrift is someone who spends, spends, and spends, whereas a tightwad is someone who doesn't spend much at all. What makes these characters different is their pain threshold. Spendthrifts find it easy to spend money, because they tend to feel relatively little pain when doing so. A tightwad likes to hold on to their money and it is possible to observe their pain as they hand it over in payment for something. Even when watching a tightwad hand over one dollar, the pain on their face is recognizable to others. This pain threshold makes it extremely difficult for tightwads to overspend or indulge themselves.

Life events may alter our spending profile, but in most instances, we are either spenders or tightwads. I personally like using these two polar extremes as examples of the types of money personalities people may have. You may find yourself somewhere in between and, depending on what is going on in your life, you may temporarily change how you spend money.

Confidence Booster
Think twice about borrowing money for short-term needs.

Some people have been spendthrifts all their lives, yet have a defining moment, like a spouse's death or job loss, and instantaneously change to the other spending profile. This profile often is rooted early in life. Consider, for a moment, what might arise if you and your partner are opposites, one a spendthrift and the other a tightwad. "Money secrets" might be common where the spendthrift does not openly share

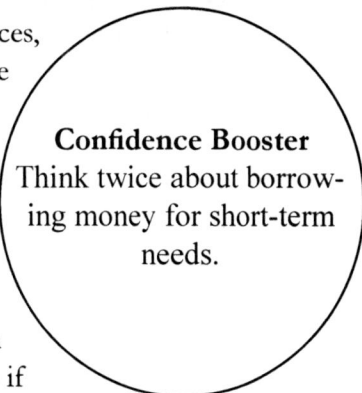

their buying habits with their tightwad partner. Conflict arises when couples start to withhold information about their spending and this can lead to a betrayal of trust. Sometimes it is easier to tell a white lie than to have to deal with the wrath of a tightwad partner.

How Rational Are You?

Scientific research shows that humans make irrational choices. Spending money on a credit card when there is not enough money to cover the expense is an example. Each of us has engaged in irrational spending behaviour, when we hope that something magical will move us out of economic helplessness and settle our bills.

We engage in what is called "temporal discounting," where we view small rewards available now, such as a new pair of shoes, as more desirable than a bigger payoff down the road in savings money for retirement. The term "temporal discounting" comes from leading researchers on Behavioural Finance. David H. Freedman wrote about "temporal discounting" in a great article in Scientific American called "Time-Warping Temptations." Researchers agree that this type of behaviour is very prevalent in the context of many bad habits such as, overeating, overspending, and drug abuse. To demonstrate the notion of "temporal discounting," an experiment was performed using student participants at The University of Pennsylvania. The students preferred to be provided with a gift certificate they could use immediately, rather than receive one that required a waiting period. Immediate gratification was preferred over even a short wait time. Impulse spending behaviour is related to the immediate availability of funds from any source - cash, credit, gift certificates - as long as the access is immediate. This experiment demonstrates how dangerous credit cards, loans, and lines of credit may be in terms of human preference for instant gratification.

When faced with making life decisions that involve money, the term "instant gratification" is opposed to mindfulness. When faced with a high-pressured salesperson, be mindful that you do not succumb to their incredible offer. Most sales strategies are designed to convince you to buy today, tomorrow, or the next day. Pause. Fast forward to imagine what your life would be like with or without the item. If you are considering buying a new $2,000 top-of-the-line bike, think about making payments month after month to afford the bike. Often we do not fast forward our minds when we make decisions. The instant gratification we feel is priceless. However, this gets deflated pretty quickly when credit card bills come in and we can`t pay them in full.

Another fascinating piece of research conducted by the University of Pennsylvania found that many of us can't envision our future selves. It is hard to fast forward twenty, thirty, or forty years. I have a difficult time seeing myself as older, because I feel so young at heart. Because we have a difficult time seeing our future selves, it makes sense that we might have a difficult time thinking about retirement and saving for it. We know it makes sense to start saving for retirement when we are young, but who can really envision their life thirty or forty years down the road? Growing old is not a process that many people want to embrace: it requires facing the reality of getting older and eventually dying. Seeing beyond tomorrow is tough. However, many people do live consciously day-to-day and are mindful about their spending, and aware of their future. They take care of their money, and also believe that the future cannot be controlled, just managed as it comes along.

When we think about our lives, it is easier to look backwards to the past for context and understanding. So when we try to fast forward and look to the future, the realm of the unknown can create discomfort. In order to grow and age mindfully, you might need to get comfortable with being uncomfortable about growing old.

Let's Make Money Real

For many people today, money is not real. This is particularly true for people who are extremely wealthy or are not worried about money.

Monopoly(R) money is the closest thing we have to pretend money. It is a rite of passage for most North American children to play the game of Monopoly. There are no real consequences to how we spend the unreal money in the game. The worst thing that can happen is fantasy bankruptcy, and being laughed at for making poor purchase decisions.

A Savvy Money Gal understands the power and realness of money.

Large numbers of us may have a very vague concept of what money really is. We are steadily progressing toward a cashless society. There are exceptions, such as children who do not yet have a debit card and teenagers who may have a debit card, but whose parents encourage them to pay for things with cash. In addition, a growing number of adults have consciously chosen to abandon the use of credit cards and pay only with cash. A significant number of elderly people visit the bank to pay their utility bills at the counter and take out cash for general expenses; they don't like to use ATM machines, credit or debit cards. So, having acknowledged these minority groups, let us address the majority of people who work and manage their money in a "paperless society." Paperless transactions are increasing every year, leading to a "buy now, pay later" approach to credit. We can tie this cashless society phenomenon to the term "instant gratification".

Nina Mazar, Associate Professor of Marketing at the Rotman School of Management, University of Toronto, and her colleague, Dilip Soman, were recently featured in an article in the Hill Times Publication called Financial Literacy is Not Enough. In the article they explain that financial literacy is not all that matters in attaining economic well-being. Economic well-being cannot be obtained without knowledge, numeracy and behavioural facilitation. They refer to this as a three legged stool in which all three legs are needed to acquire more financial success. For example, increasing your knowledge about your money is essential, this is the first leg. When we make our money a priority through honouring Personal Finance Fridays you are demonstrating your dedication to increasing your knowledge. This increase in knowledge must be balanced with the second leg, increasing your numeracy by understanding how money works, how interest is calculated on your credit card or mortgage, the time value of money etc. Finally, as you increase your knowledge and numeracy you will also begin to make better and informed choices for yourself resulting in better financial outcomes. This is the third leg of behavioural facilitation. Increasing your financial literacy requires you to increase your knowledge and change how you behave. My goal in writing this book is to help you understand that by increasing your financial literacy you can make better choices with your money and get more of what you want.

During my interview with Nina Mazar she shared additional research and insight around how technology is impacting our behaviour or choices with money. For example, cashless transactions have presented people with a new set of challenges: no one carries cash in their wallets; we rely instead on debit and credit, and conduct most of our transactions electronically. There is relatively little emotion or feeling attached to taking out a credit card or using a line-of-credit debit card from our wallets when purchasing something.

Thus, there is little pain at the point of sale. However, many of us feel the pain later when we receive our statements and find we have overspent. Sometimes we can only make minimum payments on our credit cards, or we max out our credit cards and then debt collectors start calling. We find ourselves dealing with the pain of foregoing the vacation we planned, missing out on furthering our education, or watching other goals being thwarted due to lack of funds.

Nina Mazar points out that pain has to be real before people do not repeat behaviour. It hurts when you prick your finger with a sewing needle. You soon realize that you could wear a thimble, or you could turn on a good strong light and be mindful as you sew. You need to choose a different behaviour in order not to get hurt again. This analogy holds true for money. Unless you can feel the pain of your bad money decisions, you will continue down the path of pain. We are conditioned to avoid pain in favour of activities that derive satisfaction or pleasure, but feeling pain has an important purpose in protecting us from repeating past mistakes.

Confidence Booster
Avoid marketing ploys. Advertisers understand the psychology of money.

Nina also shared additional research that her colleague Dilip Soman has conducted around behaviour modification and money. As an experiment, Dilip Soman asked a group of people to use cash for a period of time. He gave them spending money in equal amounts in four separate envelopes. What he learned was that as a person began to spend money in the first envelope, he or she became more aware (conscious) of the other three envelopes that remained. Each time a new envelope was opened, pain increased. Soman's research reveals that each time people emptied one envelope, they became more conscious about spending, and their pain threshold increased. They even took the experiment further and told people to put pictures of their children on the envelope. Let's pause for a moment and think about this research experiment and try to practically apply it to our everyday lives. How would you feel spending money on a pair of shoes instead of putting it towards your children's needs, education, and your legacy? Ouch! You may or may not open any of the envelopes. The point here is two-fold. First, people today rarely feel pain when they spend money, because most of our spending is done using debit and credit cards. And second, when faced with limited amounts of money people will make more conscious choices around our spending because parting with it causes us pain.

To see if there was any truth to the research, I tried the experiment myself. And I must admit that each time I spent the money in one envelope, I hesitated before opening the next envelope. I used to engage in mindless spending and learned my lessons the hard way. For many of us, according to Soman's research detailed above, the most difficult problems we face when it comes to money management are:

1. **We are not aware of our choices. We make mindless money decisions;**
2. **Our money and spending plan/budgeting are concepts that don't appear real;**
3. **We are removed at the point of sale from feeling the pain associated with spending.**

BMO Bank of Montreal research has indicated that, on average, Canadians spend $3,500 per year on impulse purchases and over 50% of people have buyer's remorse afterwards!

The next time you are at the grocery store, observe other people as they pay with debit or credit cards. Also observe people who pay with cash. In addition, when you go grocery shopping, be more mindful of your own behaviour. Compile your results. And, in the end, try to have a little fun with this. Laugh at your behaviour, at the choices you make.

> *"As simple as it sounds, we all must try to be the best person we can; by making the best choices, by making the most of the talents we've been given."*
> **Mary Lou Retton (1968-) Olympic Gymnast**

Keeping Money Real – Avoiding Marketing Ploys

A Savvy Money Gal is rarely tricked by others.
When we think of someone in our lives who is a spender, an image comes to mind. When we think of a Hollywood star who is a spender, an image comes to mind. We live in a consump-

tion-based culture. In the last half century, our society has moved from a savings culture to a spending culture. The earliest part of this cultural swing toward spending might have begun before World War One, but it definitely took hold after World War One during the "Roaring Twenties." It stalled during the Great Depression of the 1930s. Spending became popular again after World War Two and accelerated rapidly during the 1950s, when it was within reach for most working and middle-class households to have a "car in every driveway" and every modern electrical appliance. When the first of the boomer generation became adults in the late 1960s there was nothing stopping us. We were off to the races! During the 1970s, nobody paid much attention to the oil crisis and other drastic warnings. By the end of the 1980s, conspicuous consumption was totally obscene. And conspicuous consumption has been going full tilt ever since, for those who can afford it.

Traditionally, some marketing involves trickery; false promises are made to consumers, such as getting rich quickly, looking younger, and getting thinner. Many organizations that try to entice you to spend your money are playing on your weaknesses and vulnerability. It is easy to be persuaded to buy something when you are feeling emotionally drained or stressed. It is harder to be influenced or tricked by persuasive marketing ploys, when you are in top form. Yet, even for those who are very self-aware and mindful, the subconscious can be programmed by watching television, listening to radio, looking at billboards, and watching advertising go by on buses. Remember, "a fool and his money are soon parted."

I struggle with the same challenges as every other woman. Today, I am very self-aware of how I spend, save, invest, and gift my money. This did not happen overnight. There are always people, places, and companies that are trying to get me to part with my money. Think before you spend. While you are making someone else richer, you are making yourself poorer.

> *"Some things in life aren't even worth regretting.*
> *You're better off passing them like a*
> *freight train passes a hobo."*
> **Ethel Merman (1908 – 1984) American Actor and Singer**

The Silent Killer: Credit Card Debt

Household debt in North America is rising. Why? We are a live-for-today culture. Access to credit and low interest rates have created a perfect storm. Just walk into any major department store and you will see how easy it is to get credit. Companies entice you with the instant ten percent off your purchase.

In the United States, householders have a substantial amount of credit card debt. Of the estimated 46.7% of households that carry a balance on their credit cards, the average debt is

$15,257 as of December 2012. As reported by the Globe and Mail in a recent article (Debt by Numbers-Troubling Trends in Canadian Consumer Spending) consumer debt in Canada is also increasing at alarming rates.

It is so easy while shopping to take out your credit card to pay for things without feeling any

> *"The point is less what we choose than that we have the power to make a choice."*
> **Gloria Steinem (1934-) Feminist and Activist**

pain until the bill comes in and you don't have enough money to pay your credit card balance in full and meet your other financial obligations. When you engage in mindless spending of this nature without thinking about the repercussions or outcomes of your spending, you are setting yourself up to fail. A survey conducted by Intuit indicates that credit card debt is holding people back from getting on the road to financial success. This results in bad behaviour such as avoiding opening bills, which compounds the problem. Some are even paying their bills with a credit card. Ouch!

Money Story: Joan and Karen

Joan and Karen enjoy spending time together shopping. Joan is a tight-wad. She spends her money wisely and frugally. She is well-rounded and balanced, and would not consider herself to be an emotional shopper. She buys what she needs and is proud of the fact that she manages her money very carefully.

Karen on the other hand is a spendthrift. She has no problem spending several hundreds of dollars on purses. At today's prices, designer bags can run upwards of $500. Karen lives for today and believes in paying later. She would have little difficulty in buying a $500 purse for a special night out. She uses her credit card frequently, racks up credit card bills, doesn't pay the bills in full, and carries a balance every month. She extends her lifestyle through credit.

Envision yourself being consciously aware of having $500 in cash in your purse and heading out shopping with Joan and Karen. Who would you shop with and why?

Interest rates on credit cards are high. Paying off huge balances on credit cards over a long period of time will erode savings and destroy the chance of wealth accumulation. If you are not aware of these facts, and carry balances on credit cards, take a look at your interest payments over a period of one year. Add up that interest. Think what you could have done with that money.

> *"I have no regrets. I wouldn't have lived my life the way I did if I was going to worry about what people were going to say."*
> **Ingrid Bergman (1915-1982) Actor**

Will neighbours pay for our child's education, or help us catch up on our credit card bills, car payments and mortgage? If not, is it wise for anybody to play the "keeping up with the Joneses game"? Nowadays, the term means living beyond your means. It may be ironic to realize that the Jones family might be broke.

What Triggers Your Spending?

A Savvy Money Gal knows her spending triggers.

Let's discuss trigger points and spending. We know that indulging in simple luxuries is a sure fire way to feel good. And that "free" is always best. So let's think about how you spend your money and whether you could benefit from focusing on simpler luxuries.

Confidence Booster
Understand what triggers your spending. Next time you feel compelled to shop, think through the purchase to bill-paying time.

Understand Your Triggers

Time is well spent evaluating the various emotions, daily events, situations, and activities that might trigger bad money habits, such as overspending. When you are feeling emotional, do you find yourself geared up and ready to spend money? When you have had an argument or a stressful interaction with someone in your daily life, do you spend more? We must evaluate and identify any type of trigger that detracts from making mindful and conscious choices with our money. Once you identify your set of potential triggers, you can learn how to control them. Answer the following questions:

Do emotions influence your spending decisions?

We are well aware that emotions can trigger bad money habits. If you are in the throes of an emotion that you can identify as a possible spending trigger, be mindful and deal with that emotion. Wait until you have balanced your emotions, before you head out to shop. As funny as it may sound, having a clear mind is important when it comes to spending money.

What do you value? Define the value of everything before you make a purchase.

Does the item you wish to purchase have an emotional, financial, or spiritual value? What is it? How will it enhance your life? Is it a need or want?

_____

_____

Do you manage how you spend your money in the context of your goals? Are you investing in yourself? Spend money on goal-related pursuits.

Will the purchase in question support you achieving your future goals? If the answer is no, think twice before you spend. If the answer is yes, spend.

_____

_____

Do you know where your money is going and how you spend it? Follow the money trail.

Know where your money is going, then there will be no surprises. Most of us don't pay enough attention to how we spend our money. We forget what we buy, lose receipts, and are not careful enough when tracking our spending. If you are lost in the forest, you need to navigate to safety by means of a compass. Following your money trail is a strategy that acts as a compass and helps you stick to your spending plan.

_____

_____

Spending Plans

A Savvy Money Gal has a spending plan and reviews it on Personal Finance Fridays. She makes trade-offs on how she spends her money.

A spending plan is a tool to help you live better today, and to focus on reaching your long-term goals. In order to reach these goals you must move away from seeking benefits today and take a more holistic approach to your life. Many women attempt to adhere to a spending plan or budget, but most become discouraged and give up before the plan accomplishes any significant financial gains. If you are like most of us, it is hard to stick to a spending plan if outcomes are not quickly forthcoming. We have discussed the concept of temporal discounting in which people are more likely to engage in behaviours that yield instant gratification. The battle of the spending plan has never been more critical given the significant debt loads many families carry and the overall proclivity toward low savings rates.

The first reason why budgets fail is that we cannot form positive attitudes about setting one up. The thought of a spending plan makes us cringe. It feels too restrictive, like a financial diet, and no one likes being on a diet. You need to think outside of the box and recognize that a spending plan is a means to an end. If you appreciate your money as a resource, a spending plan is simply another tool to improve your life. Your money will enable you to achieve your personal Big Picture Goals. Creating a spending plan is an ideal way to curb buying on impulse and to increase mindful, self-aware, and authentic spending, the ingredients for increasing financial security.

The second reason why spending plans fail before they get started is that many of us lack the motivation. Ask yourself these questions: What might be my motivation for creating a budget? Am I trying to appease a partner or parent? Am I following the terms of a debt repayment plan with a consumer credit agency? These are not bad motivations, but they are external pressures and hard to maintain over time. The best motivation comes from within. Following a spending plan is self-investment in Big Picture Goals. Many women lose the motivation to adhere to a spending plan or budget because the benefits take too long to surface. Yet, by setting up a process to follow your money trail, you will know where your money is going. It is important to become fascinated with the money trail and to analyze it. Once you are able to analyze it for perhaps three months, it will be easier to understand that a spending plan does not have to be restrictive. We can use it very creatively.

A spending plan can even become a fun activity, almost like a game, where you try out various creative options. Hunting for bargains takes on a new meaning when you are holding yourself accountable to a savings plan, because a great deal of enjoyment can be derived from seeing how far you can stretch your budget. It may not take too long before you are hooked to being a tightwad!

Confidence Booster
Spend your money on simple luxuries such as life experiences. They will boost your emotional well-being and will make you happy.

The final reason why a spending plan may fail to thrive is many of us have unrealistic expectations about the process. We want immediate results. To summarize, in order to be successful in maintaining any spending plan, a good attitude, personal motivation, and realistic expectations are crucial.

Simple Luxuries – The Wise Way to Splurge

Elizabeth Dunn, the author of Happy Money, The Science of Smarter Spending is an inspiration to me in my daily life; I find myself referring to her expert research as I go about my work. Dunn extrapolates on the importance of spending money wisely in order to increase happiness. She debunks many cultural myths about what makes most people happy. I encourage you to read her book. She points out the importance of spending money on life experiences and explains that spending on others is a sure fire way to derive more satisfaction from our money.

While all the research shows us money per se does not make us happy, how can we spend it so that it does make us happy?

A Savvy Money Gal maximizes the utility and value of her money by enjoying more simple luxuries.

Simple luxuries are things in life that don't cost a lot of money, but bring happiness. What are your simple luxuries? Isn't it time you made them a priority? Not only have I empowered myself to make better choices, but I am influencing my children in a way that will benefit them for life. You won't catch me doing silly things with my money anymore.

Simple luxuries might also include physical activities that are pleasurable. Walking the dog or spending time in the park, are activities that do not cost you any money. These are some of my favourite past times—and I enjoy them as free luxuries.

Gardening has been proven to offer therapeutic benefits for many people. Not only can gardening prompt you to grow organic vegetables that are healthier for you and your family, but gardening is a soulful activity that might also provide you with benefits that are similar to meditation: serenity, relaxation, clarity, mindfulness, and self-awareness. On top of all that, you are outside and breathing fresh air!

Money, Families, and Children

A Savvy Money Gal engages her family in discussions and activities around money management.

A family that spends and budgets together shares in financial success together. It is amazing how much interest children will show in following the family money trail. They easily become engaged with discussions over the family budget because they feel very "grown-up" to be included. It is a great way to teach them how to manage money. In turn, your children may hold you accountable. Let family goals be your beacon; get all your family members involved and keep everyone informed and engaged.

Creating a spending plan with your children is an excellent way to teach them the process, so that they can set up a budget for their allowance, birthday, and odd jobs money. This will embed a good habit in them. Start early. Many parents today find it hard to find the time to teach their children about budgeting and more pleasurable to hand their children whatever money they can afford and watch them have fun with it. Further, parents may feel strongly about sheltering their children from economic realities and may honestly believe that children have plenty of time to learn about money and there is no need to rush the process prematurely. Your children benefit from learning that money is a finite resource whose utility is maximized when it is managed with attention. The more involved children become in the creation of a spending plan, the more aware they will be about making good choices with money. A spending plan will instil mindful spending habits that will take root as a "reference point" and make a life-long difference to their financial success.

A Savvy Money Gal does not shy away from difficult conversations.
Talking about money is one of the most challenging issues for each of us. When we engage in conversations about our money, we engage in conversations about our values, our livelihood, and our future. Women can talk about almost everything, like our boyfriend, partners, ex boyfriends, our weight-loss programs, but not money. Women don't talk about money - yet it is the one thing they think about all the time. Sometimes, economic jealousy can play a role in this. Perhaps a friend gets a promotion and tells you and you feel sorry for yourself, because you are making less, instead of being genuinely happy for your friend and knowing that the same positive economic boost can come your way.

Confidence Booster
Children grasp most money concepts by the ages of six and seven. Take charge of your children's futures by instilling good money principles now. They are worth it!

The American Savings Education Council conducted a survey in 2012 around children and money. They found that ninety-four percent of children look to their parents for financial guidance. The last thing any parent wants to do is to pass on bad money habits and misinformation to their children. Making intelligent money decisions and choices for our children has never been more important. Often we forget about the influence we as parents have over our children. As you go through this journey of learning better financial habits, you will become a better role model for your children and have a direct and profound impact on their lives. You will set your children up to win!

There are many experts who believe that financial literacy, which is the mechanics of money, should be taught at school. I agree that the theory should be taught at school as early as age seven, because by that age, they have grasped the majority of money concepts: what money is; how to count it; how to value it; the concept of exchanging money for goods; earning money; planning ahead; delaying an expenditure; and making choices with money.

Forging a new future around money will set your children free and on the road to financial success. Research done by the Commonwealth Bank of Australia in 2013 found that children start managing "pocket money" between the ages of four and six. The average rate is $7.17 a week. This increases to about $14.11 a week for kids aged between thirteen and fifteen. Most kids spend their money on food, snacks, and candies. For most parents, this is not what we want for our children. Only one third save their money! It begs the question, where did this behaviour come from? As a parent, think about your money values defined earlier and how you learned about money as a child. Put your children on the right path and make saving the priority, not candies.

Your children may have seen your bad money habits and past money mistakes. They might be the recipient of them in some manner. By making a conscious choice to change, you are preparing your children to be successful. There are teachable moments everyday whether you are grocery shopping, visiting the bank, using the ATM or paying bills.

If in the past you overspent and couldn't stick to a spending plan or budget, your children might already be engaging in bad money habits, depending on their age. For many mothers it is a defining moment of truth when they realize that bad habits have been passed on.

Exercises to Get Real With Your Money

The upcoming exercises will guide you toward increased utility and satisfaction with your money and to maximize the amount of money at your disposal. They will assist you to modify bad money habits that might be holding you back from obtaining more from your money. A further goal is to encourage you to face the financial consequences of bad money choices, which will free you to make increasingly self-aware good money choices.

If, after reading this chapter, you determine your spending may be out of control, please consider these few important tips. Carrying excessive debt on your credit cards will not enhance your credit rating; high debt balances will lower it. If you are having difficulty managing your credit card payments, I recommend you seek a debt consolidation loan. Usually, interest on these loans is less than you would pay on your credit card. And finally, if your financial situation has become unbearable and you are seriously concerned, debt counseling might be the best solution. Do not suffer in silent anguish; instead take action. You may be feeling ashamed, embarrassed, or foolish. I understand that. But there are some terrific people who want to help. Please Google the search term "credit counseling" and get expert, local advice.

Action Plan Exercises To Help You Get More Authentic With Your Money

1. Create a spending plan.

Without a spending plan, you will never have a good handle on your money. You won't have any idea where it is going and more importantly how to optimize what you have. Gather all your financial paperwork: bank statements, invoices, bills, and credit card statements. Put them in a pile. Download my spending planner at www.savvymoneygal.com, available on the home page, and start filling it in with your numbers. Set up your monthly spending plan, measure and track how you do. This might take you a while, particularly if you have never created a spending plan before and are not sure how you spend your money. It is a starting point, and it might take a couple of days, weeks, or even a month to truly understand where your money goes. If you don't start tracking your money trail, a spending plan will be virtually useless. This exercise is intended to increase your awareness of how you spend money.

Become more mindful when you spend money. Check in with your emotions. Think about temporal discounting. Think about your goals in the context of your spending. Your spending plan is by far one of the most important money-management strategies. It is the force behind everything you do, want and need. Without a plan, your money will be lifeless, directionless, and false. Think about how you spend your money and on what. Remember the meaning of "whole money". You no longer need to pretend to yourself with your money.

You will create your new spending plan in terms of where you want to go with your money today. You may wish to redirect money toward savings. You may decide to stop spending money on items you don't need and that only clutter your living environment.

Think about Dilip Soman's envelopes of money. Try giving yourself a monthly spending allowance in cash only and put it into four envelopes. As you go through the month, use the envelopes one by one to buy your lifestyle items. Make sure you save all receipts and immediately place them in the envelope you are currently using. Each time you deplete an envelope, write the date down, and add detail to the receipts about what you spent the money on. Watch what happens over the next month, as you spend your cash. One expected outcome is that you will start to make more conscious and aware choices. Your money will feel closer and more real. You will feel immediate pain as your cash becomes depleted from one envelope and you move on to the next. We have to go beyond financial literacy and use behaviour modification to facilitate change.

2. Start to engage in conscious choices.

When you start engaging in conscious choices, you become more mindful of how you manage and spend your money. You will think twice before you spend. Once you get into a pattern, you can move away from cash envelopes to credit and debit, but only if you trust yourself with your money. This will heighten your consciousness around how you spend your money. Another strategy to use is to tape pictures of your children on your credit cards. Next time you decide to shop with a credit card, you will think twice before spending, because you could be putting this money into their education instead.

3. Start engaging your children in discussions around money.

If they still live with you, have them help you plan the next family vacation, pay bills, and get more informed. Make this a weekly ritual; integrate it as part of your everyday life. Remember an informed child is an intelligent child. If you want your child to increase their comfort with money, share your money knowledge with them in a manner appropriate to their age.

4. Let's start forward thinking and create a vision board.

A Savvy Money Gal has a clear vision of herself and her future. It is time to think about your future and what you want to create. In order for you to be fresh and leave your past behind, I suggest we create a mental road map to where you want to go! When you start envisioning yourself in the future, you will mindfully start to make decisions that will allow you to get there.

Vision boards are a collage of images and thoughts that mentally and emotionally connect you to where you want to go in the future. They are as unique as you are. There is no specific formula or approach to take. There are no wrong vision boards. You must attach emotionally to your vision board as you create it. An intense emotional connection is the only prerequisite for a wonderful experience. Your vision board must conjure up good feelings and reflect your values, ideals, and future. Looking back at your life is not going to cut it anymore. It is important now for you to take action, and create a fresh, new, future for yourself!

Below you will find a sample of a vision board I created. It represents random thoughts and images about how I saw my future self, thinking big and dreaming big. My board helps me visualize my future in a way that helps me easily and naturally achieve what I plan for myself. Where you are today is the starting point. Your vision board is where you see yourself three to five years from now. If you are living day to day, this might be a challenge, but step outside your comfort zone and have fun!

As you create your vision board, stretch yourself to where you feel uncomfortable, but are still having fun. Consider keeping your vision board a secret, at least in the beginning. Keep in mind, once you show your vision board to somebody else, you may be held accountable to achieve the Big Picture dreams you are envisioning. You may decide to share this vision board exercise with a friend; the buddy system works very well for some people. Many people use their fridge to display their vision board. Look around your home and you may find that some personal items will trigger an idea that can be incorporated into your vision board.

To prepare for creating your vision board, ask yourself these questions:

1. Where am I today?

Are you content with your life? What areas of your life could be improved or expanded? What areas of your life need a different approach? It is important to define what "more" means to you. What does "more," mean to you, in any area of your life? Do you want to save more? Do you need more experience? Do you want more time for yourself? This is your starting point.

_____

_____

2. Where do I want to go?

If you are uncertain about how you want to improve your life, ask yourself, "what interests me?" and "what am I passionate about?" Once you have a direction, then you can create a plan and set goals that will help get you there. Remember you don't need to achieve the Big Picture overnight. Setting smaller, more realistic, and achievable goals will keep you moving forward with a positive mindset.

_____

_____

3. What is stopping me from getting where I want to go?

Many of us know exactly where we want to go in our lives, but feel stuck. There could be many reasons: a lack of money, bad money habits, self-doubt. Athletes talk about the "invisible wall" that keeps them from achieving their full potential. Unfortunately, there is no fairy dust or magic potion to tear down the wall. You can, however, break down barriers and overcome money obstacles with creativity. That means doing something differently! Ask yourself, "What invisible walls have I built?"

_____

_____

4. How have I changed successfully in the past?

The first step is always the hardest. Think back to the last time you made a successful change in your life and tap into the pride and accomplishment you felt. These feelings will help motivate you to do it again. Of course, you are bound to encounter speed bumps on your journey. The trick is to look at them as reminders that you are moving forward. List your past successes.

_____

_____

After you have answered all the questions above, give yourself time to reflect on what you have discovered. Then look around and collect images that represent your answers. Again, there is only one rule: the images must have a mental and emotional connection for you.

> _"I began to have an idea of my life, not as the slow shaping of achievement to fit my preconceived purposes, but as the gradual discovery and growth of a purpose which I did not know."_
> **Joanna Field (1900-1998) Author**

Here is a really great example of a young lawyer who completed this exercise at one of my workshops. You may find inspiration in her words.

Vision Board Preparation Example:

1. Where are you today in your life?
   Beginning to set up a family and build my career. Setting boundaries that will hopefully guide me.

2. Where do you want to go?
   Building a secure and rewarding practise – always balanced with my top priority being my family and health.

3. What is stopping you from getting to where you want to go?
   I often have competing demands on my time.

4. What qualities do you need to exhibit to get you to where you want to go?
   Patience, discipline, structure, focus, balance, and being present.

Connecting with You

1. How are you enjoying expressing your personal affirmation? Do you find it is helping you to get more focused on your goals?

    _____

    _____

2. In this chapter we spent a lot of time discussing spending, and the importance of creating a spending plan to understand where your money is going and to redirect it if it isn't being spent in a way that is optimized. Did you attempt to create a spending plan for yourself? If you have one already, what learning will you take away from this chapter that will impact your current plan?

    _____

    _____

3. Creating a vision board can be a powerful exercise. How are you making out with creating one for yourself? How did you get started?

    _____

    _____

4. How will you start actively managing your spending and engaging in conscious choices? Do you feel the power of conscious choice in its ability to making you more mindful of the decisions you are making with your life and your money?

    _____

    _____

Chapter Four ~ Strategy #4
Be Conscious of Your Life and Money Choices

"Choose well: Your choice is brief and yet endless."
Ella Winter (1898 – 1980) Journalist

Personal Learning Goal

As you read through Chapter Four, you will be encouraged to adopt conscious choice by thinking before you engage in any activity with your money. Your goal is to understand your thoughts, feelings and emotions in order to make more mindful money decisions. This will result in better financial outcomes for you and thus will increase your financial security. You will continue to develop strategies that will assist you to get very real with your life and your money. You may or may not see yourself in this chapter. I encourage you to continue reading because you may see someone you know and maybe they could use redirection. This chapter will discuss a slightly darker side of money in the context of how money can be a force of destruction, and not a tool, gift, or resource. Sometimes, spending money unconsciously helps fill a void in our life, and compensates for things we feel we are missing. We can use it to avoid talking about feelings such as loneliness, rejection, fear, isolation, or insecurity.

This chapter builds on the first three chapters of Savvy Money Gal strategies, where we spent time learning the importance of having a winning money mindset. We learned that through positive affirmations and using visualization we can create mental images for ourselves in terms of where we want to go. We also discussed the importance of looking to the future and leaving the past behind. In creating the new you, we defined what it means in today's world to find balance and be authentic. We spent some time creating a spending plan and looking to the future by engaging in a visioning exercise. When we are balanced and authentic with ourselves and our money, we spend it on simple luxuries that make us happy, rather than trying to impress other people by living a lifestyle we can't afford. This is a powerful truth. When we harness our money and direct it towards positive activities such as reaching our goals, it takes on a powerful force

The Conscious Use of Money

A Savvy Money Gal is self-aware and conscious of her choices.
The conscious use of money means using money in a purposeful way, toward long-term goals and long-term financial security. We use conscious money for principled and specific reasons. It is money that is spent with an acceptance of who you are and with an understanding that money cannot be used to take away pain or unhappiness. When you love who you are, you feel whole. You are optimistic about your future, you live with a winning mindset, and you engage in savvy money management strategies and practices. You strive to be your best and also know that, at times, good enough is good enough. You don't have to be perfect to feel complete.

Conscious money is managed money that is working for you in a way that is getting you financial results and moving you toward economic security. When you use your money more consciously, you feel a difference in your actions. Your peace of mind increases. You begin to utilize your money as a tool to enrich your life.

The Unconscious Use of Money

Many of us have used our money to make ourselves feel better. It's a common problem even if no one wants to talk about it. However, when you become very present with your thoughts and feelings in moments of hurt or anger, you have the ability to make a conscious choice of how you respond to that event. When you feel empty, engaging in an activity that gives you joy or simple pleasure is recommended. Taking a walk is a wonderful way to ground yourself and reconnect with your emotions. It doesn't cost any money and the therapeutic effects are so much greater than shopping for things you probably don't need.

Have you ever engaged in mindless spending where you went out with some friends or on your own, shopped around and bought a bunch of stuff that you realized the next day you really didn't need or want? I think each and every one of us has done this in the past, it is an illuminating example of how we can engage in mindless activities.

The Psychology of Spending

Let's spend some time digging into the psychology of spending to understand more about consumer behaviour. As we discussed earlier, many of us have spent our money in ways that have caused regret and remorse. It's not difficult to do.

Catherine Comuzzi, Ed.D., a Master Coach and Psychotherapist in private practice who specializes in trauma and change, describes the complex and conflicting relationship that can develop around money: "Money is a powerful platform from which to play out childhood insecurities.

These conflicts formed in early life, get transferred into adult life." For example, Catherine notes that those who are overly fixated on pursuing success and money may be reacting to "an earlier breach in (their) security system." She states that these "success hunters" are driven by a fear of losing. The pursuit of money is front and centre in their lives, and as a result they can lack the ability to be vulnerable and empathetic, and their relationships can take a back seat and be weakened as a result. In contrast, those who defend against and keep at bay feelings of defeat and disappointment can develop a neglect of money issues in an attempt to not have to deal with their emotions. As Catherine maintains, those who neglect money may feel valueless and be waiting for someone else to provide for them financially. They lack clarity and discernment and "have not learned to respect or protect their interests or work towards their goals."

Catherine identifies a range of emotional types and accompanying neurotic money habits: "the success hunter, the gambler, the gold-digger, the playboy, the miser, the embezzler, the impostor, the dependent and helpless, the bargain-hunter and the seekers of windfalls and easy money." Whichever type you may be, and to whatever degree, it is important to be self-aware and recognize your money habits and come to terms with the emotional driving force. Then you can start applying money management strategies suited to your particular situation, developing a mature and wiser approach to your money.

Emotional Shopping

Research tells us that a negative mood is the precursor to spending money through emotional shopping. Emotional shopping differs from compulsive shopping. Emotional shopping can be compulsive when it occurs repeatedly, but it can also be occasional. All of us have engaged in emotional shopping where we spend money to feel better. We shop to fill a void. Repeated cycles of emotional shopping can lead to huge bills and debts that can be difficult to control. Emotional shopping is one of the biggest challenges people have when it comes to managing their money. This is a bad habit most of us have engaged in. It can derail our financial future and hinder us from achieving our goals. It might go something like Susan's story.

Money Story: Susan

Susan is a thirty-something gal who is constantly fighting with her partner about money. Why? There could be a thousand reasons, but over the past few years they have had a very bumpy relationship. Each time they get into an argument, Susan heads over to shop to get some retail therapy. She spends hundreds of dollars on her credit cards and buys things she doesn't really need. This lifeless money spending gives her a temporary lift and makes her feel better. The next day, she wakes up and realizes that she has overspent and can't afford what she bought.

In addition, she makes up with her partner and everything feels good again until the next argument, when the cycle starts all over again.

Susan is a compulsive shopper; she can't pass up a good bargain. She knows she has a problem with overspending but can't stop; her compulsive shopping is ongoing. Susan buys things to make herself feel better—she spends "feel good money." She engages in a daily ritual of emotional shopping. Her closets are packed with new clothes; many items still have their price tags on. She has racked up credit card bills, and has difficulty paying them down. She is often late with her rent money and uses her credit card to pay for her essential items including groceries. Susan has tried many times to stop her binge shopping and has had some success, but often reverts back to the same old habits.

Susan's doctor referred her to a psychologist to help her deal with her emotional shopping problem and unearth the cause of it. Interestingly enough, her shopping binges didn't start out with daily shopping. They escalated over the years to uncontrollable behaviour. Susan suffered trauma early in her life and has had a difficult life since childhood. She never got over the trauma, and shopping became a way to heal her deep pain and soothe her emotions. Susan is not a bad person, yet her choices have resulted in both emotional and financial consequences. I am happy to say Susan has made a courageous decision to go into counselling and work through her challenges, in order to feel better and become whole again.

At this point it is completely clear, compulsive shopping is different from merely emotional shopping. Compulsive shopping is emotional shopping taken to the extreme. There are some conditions in life that can trigger an occasional emotional shopper into becoming a hard-core compulsive shopper. This is a serious matter and cannot be minimized. It usually requires professional help to mitigate. I fully support seeking counsel from doctors and psychologists who can help.

Economic Jealousy

Economic jealousy can make women and men act in self-sabotaging ways by overspending to seek an elevated status. Many women become jealous of other women for their perceived economic success. Jealousy can debilitate you and stop you from moving forward. If you find yourself feeling jealous, perhaps not specifically toward an individual, but perhaps simply in general toward people who appear to have status and economic success, it is important you recognize immediately that you are letting your insecurities and self-doubt gain control of your thoughts, feelings, and emotions. Some believe

Confidence Booster
Jealousy comes from faulty thinking that you can't get something you want that someone else has. A winning mindset will squash the negative energy jealousy can create.

jealousy is a great motivator. I disagree. I believe a healthy competitive spirit can be a powerful motivator and propel us to want and get more. But why be jealous about a success that you are perfectly capable of achieving yourself? There is no disputing the fact that it is difficult when there are unequal economic successes in families and between long-standing good friends. Managing the differences becomes a task requiring skillful and highly refined emotional intelligence.

If you are the recipient of economic jealousy, it is important to resolve your feelings and try and hold on to the happy memories of the relationship, while guiding your friend or family member to a better understanding of your success. You may be achieving success, but you also don't want to be alone in that success, so you may have to convince your friend, or relative, that they are really valuable and important to you. This may take extra time and effort, and for some of you it may not work. If your friend or family member is completely and repeatedly cruel to you, try to distance yourself a bit and welcome them back when they make an effort to change. Remember, they may keep their distance until they have a success they can proudly bring to you. If this is the case, provide them with the enthusiasm that was denied you; this will strengthen your relationship in the long run. Try not to slam a door shut if at all possible. Who said long-term friendships and family relationships were easy and never had to go through rough spots?

Recall in previous chapters we discussed that money may buy things but it does not buy happiness. More money does not necessarily equate with more happiness. People value money differently and are at different levels in enhancing their money management skills. Money jealousy can cause problems in relationships. It is very destructive and it is one of those emotions that needs to be redirected to a more positive state. Say your best friend's husband is an executive with a Fortune 500 company, be happy for her. Don't silently begrudge her for the perceived success that comes with being the wife of a corporate executive. Or if your best friend gets a promotion with a very large raise or a terrific year-end bonus, try not to begrudge her for her success. You have the same ability to find success by embracing a winning mindset and following the strategies presented in this book.

> "You gain strength, courage and confidence by every experience in which you really stop to look fear in the face. You are able to say to yourself, I have lived through this horror. I can take the next thing that comes along. You must do the thing you think you cannot do."
> **Eleanor Roosevelt (1884-1962) Former First Lady of the United States**

Perfectionism in Women

A Savvy Money Gal accepts her imperfections.

Perfectionism relates to 'money' and its use. Some women put far too much pressure on themselves in the pursuit of happiness, joy and meaning in life. Perfection does not exist except in math problems. Trying to have a perfect life is not possible. This does not mean that a woman should never strive to be the best possible version of herself. It does mean that it is necessary to be moderate in your expectations, both of yourself and others.

If you set perfection goals for yourself that are too lofty or unattainable you will set yourself up for failure and disappointment. It is important to remind yourself that you don't need to be in control all the time to live by a higher code of living; you can manage your money for improved outcomes. Don't set yourself up with expectations that are inflexible. You want to be happy with your money management results; set your goals within reasonable limits and time frames. Don't seek perfection, because at times good enough can be good enough. Strive to find the balance between happiness and success while always putting your best effort into your many roles, whether it's that of a partner, a mom, a sister, a co-worker or a friend. Continue to consider what role perfection plays in your life as it applies to your money habits and maintain balanced, reasonable expectations.

Fear

A Savvy Money Gal is brave and resilient.

Fear is one of the most debilitating emotions. Fear typically falls into two categories: fear of success and fear of failure. Fear easily overwhelms women, leading to self-sabotage in ways that can lead to bad outcomes. Think about what you are really afraid of in life in the context of your money. Are you afraid of appearing unknowledgeable or of making the wrong decisions with your money? Many women cling to fear and use it as an excuse for not investing in the stock market because they have, or they know someone else who has, experienced a large financial loss through stocks and they are fearful of the same fate. Others fear having to relinquish control of their money in a multitude of ways. The point here is to recognize the role fear plays in your life and to manage this fear as it relates to your money. People engage in two polar emotions – love and fear. Once a person gravitates toward fear-based decision making and fear-based influences, they have lost value and grounding in self-love and they have closed their minds to the possibility of other perspectives.

> *"The only real prison is fear, and the only real freedom is freedom from fear."*
> **Aung San Suu Kyi (1945) Human Rights Activist and Political Leader**

Fear and the lack of perceived success and apparent accomplishment are at the heart of why many women don't talk about money and remain silent. Why do we let fear take hold? Fear is paralyzing. Fear comes from living in the past. It is not a forward-moving emotion, because it is full of negative energy. Having some level of fear is natural for all of us, but when fear becomes an overriding emotion, it can stunt growth. Fear must be managed and directed in order to get to a new and better place.

Many women fear going into debt counseling and see it as a sign of failure rather than redirection. Seeking professional help during such a trying time is paramount to learning about more empowering money management strategies. This is just the beginning. Addressing debt is the first step to a long journey to recovery and to managing money in better ways. Taking debt counseling or going to a financial institution to discuss overspending or debt consolidation loans is the required action. Please don't feel shame or embarrassment. Some financial institutions may not be sympathetic to your debt situation. You may be fearful of rejection. Address your fear by visiting your financial institution with a more positive attitude and remind yourself of the end goal of getting out of debt. Once you have a debt plan in place you will be able to redirect yourself toward engaging in more goal setting and getting back on track financially. It may take time to strengthen your self-belief and move beyond the emotional pain you may feel. You will eventually get there. Leaving past money mistakes behind, as we discussed earlier, is a freeing and liberating process. Once you get back on a path to more financial security, please be mindful of your past and the triggers that got you into trouble with spending and debt.

Deep Wounds

A Savvy Money Gal believes in healing past hurt.

There are some people who live their entire lives carrying baggage from their youth. We discussed earlier the importance of leaving the past behind and starting afresh. A wound might be connected to the past behavior of your parents or guardians. A wound could be so great that it interferes with the everyday functioning of the individual who is afflicted. For some people, the wound originates from rejection or abandonment by a parent. When a parent has very poor self-esteem, or minimal self-love, their feeling of unworthiness may be passed on to their child. This is referred to as a "hole in the soul." This wound might manifest itself in self-destructive money behaviour. Money is used to soothe the wound and to increase self-esteem and self-image, to allow the wounded one to appear powerful, confident, and in control. This is a superficial bandage that will not heal the wound. This is also referred to as having a false sense of self. If you have deep wounds that you feel you cannot manage on your own, redirection is possible with professional help.

A Savvy Money Gal sees her behaviour for what it is.

If you find yourself engaging in destructive behaviour with your money, acknowledging this is a starting point. Know this can happen to any one of us. Redirect yourself by engaging professionals who specialize in helping people manage behaviours like overspending, such as a credit counsellor. Or if you find your wounds are really deep, and you are engaging in unconscious acts of spending to feel better, a psychologist might be able to help you deal with the original pain and trauma that is causing you to engage in destructive behaviours that are holding you back from success.

Connecting with You

1. How do you think you will use the techniques of increasing your consciousness about money to know yourself better today? How do you feel about the concept of conscious choice and being more mindful with your money?

   _____

   _____

2. Check in with your thoughts and emotions before you head out to go shopping – how do you feel and what goes through your mind? Be mindful of the fact that a bad mood is generally a precursor to impulse shopping, so check your emotions at the door. Remember, spending your money must not be a thoughtless act.

   _____

   _____

3. How are you progressing with creating your spending plan? Did you engage in some fun when creating your vision board?

   _____

   _____

Chapter Five ~ Strategy #5
Organize Your Life and Money

"Disciplining yourself to do what you know is right and important, although difficult, is the highroad to pride, self-esteem, and personal satisfaction."
Margaret Thatcher (1925- 2013) Former Prime Minister of the United Kingdom

Personal Learning Goal

You are well on your way to understanding yourself and to embracing a new you with the Savvy Money Gal Strategies. With these strategies your money problems will diminish. You will learn to organize your money in ways that will give you peace of mind and free up time to spend on what matters to you. You will know what you value and how to find more balance in your life. Your emotional well-being will get a giant boost.

This chapter is quite exciting as we will build on the idea of conscious choice and the power of being mindful before engaging in any financial activity. It's all about making better decisions and achieving better financial outcomes. We worked through strategies to help you get real with your life and money. We looked at some of the unconscious choices we make to avoid pain. Having a winning mindset and believing that you deserve good things in life is empowering. We are consciously and actively now engaged in looking to the future. As we harness our money and direct it toward positive activities such as reaching our goals, money takes on a powerful force of energy that becomes almost unstoppable.

Clutter-Free Life. Clutter-Free Money.

A woman's emotional well-being can get a boost from being more organized. Reduced spending leads to less clutter and to a healthier and happier life as a result.

Not being organized creates both emotional and financial impacts. When your money and your life are organized, you are on purpose and focused, and spending your money in a disciplined and streamlined manner that leads to peace of mind. A home that is too full of material possessions often is a sign of overspending. This is when clutter occurs; money is wasted on stuff that eventually ends up in landfills. When you are on purpose and have a clear focus, you are organized, mindful, and self-disciplined.

Waste Not, Want Not

Clear space, equating with a clear mind, is never more evident than when it comes to getting your home organized. It is often under the best and the worst of circumstances that a professional organizer is called in to assist in navigating the emotional journey of getting one's home organized. Whether it's the addition of a new baby to the family, the blending or break-up of a relationship, the downsizing of a family home, or the loss of a loved one, the one common element that people crave for is more space to stow away their stuff!

While there is the inevitable physical dilemma of trying to manage a household that is bursting at the seams with all its possessions, the emotional and financial tolls are the hidden dangers we often ignore.

Money Story: Sarah

The following Money Story was shared by Linda Chu, a professional organizer based in Vancouver, who is the founder of Out of Chaos: Professional Organizing Solutions:

Sarah's parents had lived in their home for over fifty years. Like most parents of their generation, "waste not, want not" was the motto, meaning "don't waste what you have and you will never lack anything."

Sarah moved back into her parents' home after her mother's passing. Since Sarah was single and had no children, the house was too big for her to manage on her own. She wanted to sell, since it would fetch a good price in the current real estate market. Her intention was to lean out the rooms- rooms full of personal possessions and a lifetime of collections- so that she could put the house up for sale. That intention is now five years old.

In the five years since her mother passed, Sarah has found herself immersed in the memory of each inanimate object. Her intention of clearing the decks became an emotional battle of living down memory lane and, at times, Sarah became consumed by guilt about letting go of items that "meant something" to her parents, despite the fact that they had little intrinsic value.

Try as she would, it was almost impossible for Sarah to clear away anything, not even items that had no value to her, whether it was yards of fabric purchased by her seamstress mother, or the decades of old newspaper clippings saved by her father. Compounding the situation was all that Sarah had collected in just five years since taking over the home. Her collection of magazine subscriptions, including Cooking Journals, Reader's Digests and endless ideas for scrapbooking – were mostly never read and still in their delivery pouches. She must have had at least five magazine subscriptions, not counting the Hello Magazines and anything with 'Special Edition' that she purchased at the grocery store.

Consider for a moment the financial cost to Sarah over the five years. If she had sold the house five years earlier and invested the money, what would be the value of this money today?

If you add up all the magazine subscriptions and incidental magazine purchases she had made over five years, how much money had she spent on unread materials?

Sadly it was her own health crisis that led Sarah to reach out to enlist the help of the professional organizing company run by Linda Chu, Out of Chaos: Professional Organizing Solutions. Sarah finally accepted that she needed help. She realized that despite the emotional attachment to her parents' home, she did not have the physical capacity or the financial means to maintain such a large home, especially once she started to consider her dream of taking a trip every year.

Even though she engaged a real estate agent to sell the house, it could not be listed in its current condition. It was not show-worthy for an open house. This was the ammunition Linda's company needed to help Sarah work through the physical possessions that trapped her in her home. Sarah was ready to let go. She was open to working with a team of professional organizers to go through room by room and item by item and make some hard decisions.

For Sarah, letting go meant:

- Hiring a 3 to 7 person team each day
- Tallying 9 days of labour
- Yielding 300 person-hours
- Requiring 4 trailer-loads of removal
- 9 hours moving
- 1 five-ton truck
- 10x20 foot storage locker

Sarah's home was now clear enough for cleaners to come in; and for the home to be prepared for sale. However, once the house sells, Sarah would still have to find ways to pack all her items.

She rented a storage locker, at a monthly rate of $400.00 per month ($4800.00 annually) to store away items that she was just not ready to let go of. At least 150 boxes in storage were full of books and magazines. Most of the items in storage however would not fit into the new, smaller home that Sarah would eventually buy. How many months or years of rental do you think Sarah will incur as she slowly sorts through each packed box to decide which item can be moved into her new home, and which item she can let go of?

Consider for a moment what items you are holding onto in your life. What is the financial cost of your emotional attachment to items that you likely will never use or even remember you had?

A Savvy Money Gal is self disciplined.

She enjoys the best that life has to offer, but she is also very aware of the trap of collecting things that leads to a cluttered life. When she lives a clutter-free life, she is organized and finds more financial security—living with increased happiness, energy, and power. When our money is organized, it is money that is streamlined and managed. It has vision, purpose, and a future. We feel more empowered and organized. We find more time to do the things that matter in our lives. We are not scattered or consumed by clutter. When you engage in clutter-free money, you have fewer bank accounts, fewer credit cards, and fewer paper statements. You let technology do the work for you by conducting most of your banking electronically. You worry less about your money, because you know you have money in your accounts. Bills are paid on time and you no longer pay excessive amounts of interest on your credit cards, because you use them only for convenience. You live an authentic life that is clutter-free. You have streamlined your environment and space, and no longer feel overwhelmed by your surroundings and life. The clutter and chaos is gone, replaced with simplicity and functionality.

A Savvy Money Gal's surroundings are clutter-free.

Clutter can consist of many different things that you have no use for and have been accumulating for a long time. Many of us have learned from our parents and grandparents to keep things "just in case." This "saving and keeping", a war time mentality, is a sentiment of a past when everything was rationed and personal belongings were treasured. Today, we live in a world of clutter that has accumulated from conspicuous consumption. Stuff is cheap. Often, we think we will have some use for something down the road such as a pair of shoes we haven't worn in years or a skirt we used to love. The reality is that nine out of ten times we will never use the item again.

So why do we do this? There are two main reasons why women tend to collect a lot of clutter. One reason is that we feel we have something of value and continue to hang on to items that, in reality, have very little or no value. Often women feel an emotional connection to something, which makes it hard to let go of. Similar to Sarah, we might find it difficult to let go of things associated with our past. Letting go means closure and moving forward, and sometimes we are not ready to let go of our past. But as we learned in Chapter Two, leaving your past behind and starting afresh is the only way to find more financial security. Living in the past will keep you stuck. Some women are afraid to throw things out, fearing they might need it later. In more serious cases, someone may have a compulsive disorder that compels them to keep everything they receive, even junk mail and newspapers, just in case they may want to look at them some day.

Money Story: Jenny

Jenny had accumulated so much stuff in her house that it started to cause problems with her marriage. Her husband desperately wanted to renovate their home, because it was dated. Instead of paying the high transaction costs of moving and selling the family home, renovation seemed the best option.

However, over the years, Jenny had accumulated rooms full of stuff: her parents' old furniture and belongings, her children's outgrown clothes and stuffed toys. Jenny knew what she had to do, but could not get herself to get rid of the clutter that was linked to her past. She lived in the past and was unable to move forward because time had frozen for her. Jenny couldn't let go of anything.

Being stuck in the past can have emotional and financial impacts. Even if the family decided to sell the house instead of renovate, they would still have to deal with the clutter. Jenny's husband stepped in and hired a professional organizer who was able to help Jenny deal with the emotional connection she had to material items, and to help her simplify and streamline her home. It was not an easy task. She spent time evaluating what was really important to her and in the end she found that almost 80% of the material possessions she had kept really didn't mean much. She was able to redirect her feelings and thoughts toward more positive actions. She took pictures of the old furniture and home accessories she would no longer keep, and created a photo book of memories. With the help of her personal organizer, she was able to release a lot of emotion she had tied to material items and redirect herself in a more positive and forward-moving manner.

There is no quick fix to getting clutter-free in your life. All of us hold on to material items of the past, because they represent deep emotional attachments to a time in our life or to a person who mattered. However, holding onto objects that only have emotional value can keep you from moving forward. I am not suggesting that you relinquish every sentimental item from your past, but you are going to have to make a conscious choice in terms of what really has value. The following suggestions will help you get more clutter-free in your space.

How to get Clutter-Free

Evaluate your clutter.

Identify items that have true value to you. This will require some time and some soul searching because you may not be able to easily decide. Think about whether the item will have value in the future. Value could mean you will have a use for it, or its value may be intrinsic or sentimental. Even if you will not use them in the future, you may want to keep your sentimental items safe and secure. For instance, you may have keepsakes created by your children that you will never wish to part with. I keep all of my son's artwork, because I value it dearly.

Define value.

Everything in life has some form of value. It is important to define the type of value each item has in your life. When you look at your things, think about whether the item has sentimental or financial value, or perhaps a mixture of both. Only you can decide this and once you do you will be in a better position to organize the items. Some items may be pure junk and ready for the trash can.

Give away unwanted items.

Feel good about giving things away to those who may have a need for them, through organizations such as Goodwill, the Salvation Army, or a women's shelter. This will take some planning and organization in terms of who could most benefit from what you have to give. Let go of the past.

When you are sorting through your items, have some objectivity. You might be holding on to things that really don't mean anything to you today. Much like releasing old money values, letting go of clutter is liberating. Leaving the past behind is healthy and will allow you to move forward and get to where you want to go. You may want to engage a friend to help you sort through your items. Don't just throw away everything for the sake of getting organized. By redirecting yourself away from the past and toward the future, you will be able to let go of old furniture, clothes, shoes, toys, and books, that really have no meaning in your life. You can also redirect by creating a scrapbook.

Implement a two-year rule.

If you find clothing in your drawers, cupboards, or closets that you have not worn in two years, the likelihood of wearing them again is slim. Part with the item. Sell it or give it away.

Shift your mindset.

Organizing your life and space will give you inner calm and more time for yourself. With a more balanced environment, you will be less distracted by the past. The energy from your clutter-free home will propel you forward.

If you want to free yourself of clutter, you have to change your behaviours and become more consciously aware of how you are spending your money. Are you spending your money to accumulate more stuff? You will have to learn to evaluate everything before you buy it. If you squander your money on stuff you don't need, how will you have enough money to reach your goals? You won't. Becoming clutter-free is really a mindset shift where you move away from finding value in things toward living more authentically. You will be free to enjoy the simple luxuries and pleasures in life that will fulfill you more than meaningless material possessions.

The Rise of Thrift

There is currently a global trend towards less conspicuous consumption and the rise of thrift. By this I mean people are becoming far more mindful about waste and clutter, and to that end, material items are being repurposed with little financial cost or impact. The term "liquid life" has been used to refer to the extension of life for material goods. For example, bikes, toys and books may be sold or given away as second-hand items several times over to many different people over their lifetime.

In addition, the barter economy is growing, in which people are exchanging goods and services with each other with no exchange of money. For example, someone may be a hairstylist and provide their services for someone in exchange for babysitting services.

These global shifts in consumer behaviour are creating a new economy, the "Cinderella economy", where people are buying lifestyle but are living within their means. "Renting lifestyle" encompasses such things as renting cottages, homes, cars, boats etc., for a short period of time instead of purchasing them and going further into debt. People are "renting lifestyle" when they want and need it, at a fraction of the monetary cost or in some cases with no exchange of money. This trend may eventually replace the need to keep up with the Joneses – the desire to buy things on credit we can't afford- the attempt to get the lifestyle without the financial commitment. Thank goodness!

Managing Yourself

A Savvy Money Gal manages herself.

The first step to becoming clutter-free is to keep the end goal in mind: the freedom it will provide you emotionally and financially. Becoming clutter-free encompasses a wide spectrum and includes everything from freeing your mind of old thoughts and feelings from the past, to freeing your space and surroundings of clutter. When you create a personal space that is clutter-free, you are creating a forward-moving path. And when an unexpected life event occurs you will be able to manage it better because you have inner calm and peace.

A Savvy Money Gal manages her time with precision.

The second step to becoming more clutter-free is to manage your time with the utmost care. Time is the most valuable commodity each of us has, but sometimes we waste it on activities that produce zero return. When you don't manage your time, you don't manage your life. We can't buy time but what we can do is optimize our time by using it wisely. Each and every one of us wishes we could have a twenty-fifth hour in the day to do all the things we need to do. So before we go any further, start considering honestly how you manage your time.

Ask yourself these simple questions:

1. How organized am I in terms of my life, my home and my money?

_____

_____

2. Do I use my time wisely and effectively or easily give it away to others without thinking?

_____

_____

3. If I had more time what would I be doing differently? What more would I accomplish?

_____

_____

4. What one thing could I do differently to help manage my time better?

_____

_____

If you are like most women, the answers to these questions probably don't surprise you. The wonderful thing about our journey is that at any time along the way we can redirect our thoughts and activities to get to a more positive place. The phrase "time is money, money is time" comes from the Ancient Greeks. Your time is valuable. If you had to put a price tag on it, what would it be? What would an hour of your time be worth? I want you to think about your time in terms of dollars. Next time you are faced with making a decision on how you are going to spend your time, keep this dollar figure in the back of your mind. A paramount shift will occur when your time has monetary value. Sometimes it pays to hire someone to do something for you, because your time is too valuable. Many women complain about the time it takes to clean their homes. Perhaps the time is better spent by hiring someone to do it for you and redirect your time to some other task. How you manage your time can make the difference between having a good life and having a great life. If you are wasting your time on activities that do not align with your goals, you will not move ahead. What is your time really worth? Think about it.

Stay-at-home moms who do not receive a formal paycheque from work may have trouble valuing their time. In 2012, Time Magazine published an article on the value of the work of a stay-at-home mom. Their findings were clear. Stay-at-home moms put in a work week of 94.7 hours, worth an average hourly rate of $17.80 or $112,962 per annum. This takes into account all of the responsibilities: cooking, shopping, cleaning, organizing the family's activities, educating, personal care. When actual work hours are examined, stay-at-home moms worked 57.9 hours a week, which translates to $66,979 per annum. This point illustrates the value of time. If you are a stay-at-home mom and know how time flies because you are always busy, you will not be surprised by this, but make no mistake: your time is of tremendous value to your family and to society.

A Savvy Money Gal lives by her values.
Value-based decision making will help you focus on spending time on what matters. When you are faced with making decisions in your life, you must stay on purpose and align with your values. When you align your activities and decisions to your values, you create inner harmony and have less conflict between your heart and mind. Here are some suggestions to help you define your core personal values to help guide and even redirect you when faced with an activity or a request for your time. Each and every one of us has in the past wasted our time on activities that have consumed our energy with little payback or return. Becoming more mindful of your time and what you do with it will give you greater clarity.

Finding More Balance in Your Life

All of us have stress in our lives. Stress comes from feeling overwhelmed. In small doses it can be good if it inspires you, resulting in productivity and achievement. However, chronic stress can affect your physical and emotional health, and over time it takes its toll. Stress is a result of feeling a lack of control in your life. The first step to diminishing stress is to take back control of your life and manage your calendar as we discussed earlier.

If your job is causing you anguish and stress all the time, it may be time to reconsider your professional position. In my life, one of the best decisions I made while working in the corporate world was to reduce my hours to part-time. My priorities in life took a dramatic shift when I became a mother. I wanted to participate in my son's life. My workplace valued my decision and I had the best of both worlds. I maintained an excellent corporate job, while being able to participate more in my son's life. My reduced pay was offset by the money I saved on childcare expenses and travel. I took control over my life and the money followed.

Remember that work-life balance is not just a question of the hours you spend in one place or the other. It is also a question of how balanced you feel and how you react to your life. How you respond to anything in life will determine your success.

Even with a managed calendar you may feel you are lacking balance in your life. You may have to consider letting go of something. In 2012, Professors Linda Duxbury and Christopher Higgins surveyed 25,000 Canadians in their 2012 National Study on Balancing Work and Care Giving in Canada. Their findings revealed people are overworked and that pressure and tension are taking a toll on emotional well-being:

> "Almost two-thirds of us are working more than 45 hours a week – 50-per-cent more than two decades ago. Work weeks are more rigid, with flex-time arrangements dropping by a third in the past 10 years. To top it off, only 23 per cent of working Canadians are highly satisfied with life. That's half as many as in 1991."

Workplace roles place a higher strain on women who, despite having primary or equal responsibility to provide the family income in almost half the families surveyed, are still largely the primary caretakers of children. More than half of the survey's respondents took work home with them, putting in an average of seven extra hours a week from home. Nearly two-thirds spent more than an hour a day catching up on emails; one-third spent more than one hour emailing on their days off.

The study also found that the less affluent a family was, the more likely it was to feel burdened by excess workloads.

One-third of participants in the research found that overloaded work and family responsibilities had a high tendency to cause them to lose sleep or dramatically reduce their energy levels. Even some of the most powerful and famous people in the world struggle with balance. Michelle Obama stated in an interview in 2013:

> "I personally… know the challenges of leading a busy life at work and at home, trying to do a good job at both — and always feeling like you're not quite living up to either — and trying not to pit one against the other, really trying to balance it…I call myself a 120-percenter…If I'm not doing any job at 120 percent, I think I'm failing."

There is a huge generational divide in the workplace today. Baby Boomers are used to working long hours, 70-80 hours a week. Generation X and Millennials value their time differently and have a different approach to working long hours. They are generally more conscious of trying to maintain a work-life balance. Who has the right approach?

The Gen Y or the Millennial group of twenty-and thirty-something-year-olds are changing the landscape of the working world – if they are able to find jobs after college or university. A recent study indicates that many Millennials are choosing to turn down promotional opportunities in favor of greater work-life balance.

Most of this group of young adults were raised in families where both parents worked and they experienced the sacrifices and demands placed upon their parents firsthand. Not surprisingly, of all the generations in the workforce today, these young adults are the most likely to consider job flexibility and schedules when they look for a job, which in turn is key to employee retention for companies.

If you think that work and family life balance is a small problem, you may be interested to know that in addition to the few companies that have recognized the issue and taken the lead in establishing work-life balance programs, there are numerous organizations, foundations, universities, and groups doing research on this topic. They are looking at the long-term effects of overload and lack of balance in our lives. Society is just scratching the surface in understanding the true toll of leading an unbalanced life.

Many researchers have studied the evolving issues connected to overwork and lost community connections. While the implications of an unbalanced work-life are numerous, they all share a common outcome. Living an unbalanced life where work dominates your time can affect your health detrimentally. Long or stressful work hours can cause problems with your heart, blood pressure, and sleep cycles. Most of us know someone who is constantly suffering from health issues, taking many sick days, or on stress leave. Having good health is a form of wealth. An unbalanced life, which is void of time and personal energy, is creating a perfect storm for many women. If you are feeling exhausted and have little time for yourself, your health is bound to suffer. When you spend all your time at work, your emotional reserves become depleted. You have no patience or ability to give to those you care about in a way that creates meaning and joy. Balance must be a goal for all of us.

Confidence Booster
Spend your time on activities that give you 100% return on your personal investment.

Organizing Your Time

Being effective and maximizing your day is about using your time efficiently. You must spend your time as wisely as you spend your money and manage it with precision. Money and time are limited resources. They are finite, yet we often give away our most precious resources in ways that do not benefit us.

Start getting organized by planning a consistent routine of activities every morning and every week. This will help you focus better at work, and manage your family life better. The most precious gift any of us could get is the gift of time- to do more and get more accomplished. Acquiring new habits that will set you on the road to daily success will help you find more balance and calm. I guarantee it. There is nothing worse than being frazzled in the morning. Organizing yourself daily will help you achieve more. Managing your time is the recipe for getting ahead personally and financially.

A Savvy Money Gal who is a Mother, manages "Mother Guilt".

Please, do not let "Mother Guilt" get the better of you. You deserve and need time for yourself to get more grounded and focused. Take the time to plan well, and use a simplified calendar to create an organized life that you manage and control. How will you optimize your day-to-day life and get more control over how you spend your time? First, let's start with a calendar. You can use your cell phone, download a calendar online or buy a paper calendar. Whatever you do, you must carry your calendar with you at all times, other than during family time and personal free time. Your calendar must become a core personal management tool in your life, to look at and review all the time.

> **Confidence Booster**
> Saying "no" will actually boost your emotional well-being. Just get over the guilt.

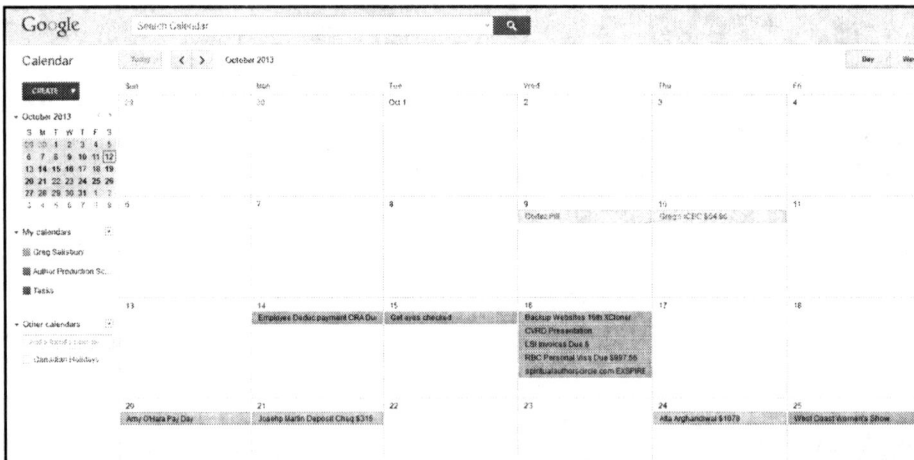

A Savvy Money Gal lives by her calendar.

Create a calendar that serves as a weekly tool. Each day should have time slots, and each and every slot should be full, including time for yourself. Every activity should be fully accounted for. Even your spare time and time you need to drive your children to an after-school program or class. Why? In this way you learn to manage your time and take control of how you spend your time. And before you accept a new task or activity you have to check in with your calendar to see if you have time. If you have to give up something on your calendar, you will have to

> *"It is not easy to find happiness in ourselves, and it is not possible to find it elsewhere."*
> **Agnes Reppler (1855-1950) American Essayist**

evaluate how it will work for you. In doing this, you will stay true to your priorities. When you manage your calendar you manage yourself. The purpose of this exercise is to demonstrate the importance of managing your time. Most women complain they don't have enough time in the day, but can't account fully for how they spend their time. Creating a calendar will do wonders for you.

An optimized calendar means that you account for your time. Use color-coded activities so you can differentiate between work, family, professional appointments, etc. Fill your calendar with activities you manage. This will effectively control how you spend your time when new requests are made of you. You will have to make the conscious choice either to give up something on your calendar or to say "no". I am sharing this approach to time management as one way to fully optimize your time. If you can manage your time with this type of precision, you will get more done, you will save time, and I can guarantee that you will save money.

The Power of Saying "No"

A Savvy Money Gal feels confident saying "no".

Saying "no" is difficult for women, but we must learn to say "no" in order to stay focused on our key priorities. It is so easy to get side-tracked doing things that may not align with your goals and your future. We all do it. Women really do have a difficult time saying "no," but we must learn its power.

A Savvy Money Gal manages financial stresses through creative problem solving.

Financial stress and burdens are taking their toll on North Americans. Many people are burdened with high debt that could be taking a toll on their health, well-being, and happiness. This debt stems from the "live for today" culture, as well as from consumerism and materialism.

Having clutter-free money is a state of organization. It means paying your bills on time; reconciling your accounts; knowing where your money is going; and creating a system that allows you at any given moment to know how much you have, and where you have accounts. It also means embracing financial strategies that will protect and increase your financial security.

Here are some practical ways to harness your day-to-day money and to become clutter-free:

1. Live by your spending plan. Know where you and your money are going. Keep track of your spending and balances in your accounts. Always maintain a minimum balance in your accounts. Never go into overdraft because it is costly, and will erode your savings.
2. Carry only one credit card. This will make reconciling your spending plan easier and allow you to better manage your credit with credit agencies.
3. Have only two personal accounts: a savings and a chequing account. If you are in a relationship as part of a couple, find a balance in terms of the number of accounts you have as a couple.
4. Keep track of and record all your personal information. This includes account information, account numbers, financial institutions etc., and put a copy of this document in your safety deposit box. If the unexpected happens, you will be prepared.
5. Put a system in place for paying all your bills electronically. This can be done through automatic payments. You will pay bills on time and face no more late fees and interest.
6. Keep all your receipts. This includes for items and activities such as groceries, school trips, clothes, and books. Put the receipts in a monthly folder. Reconcile your spending plan monthly to see if you are staying on track. If you overspend, adjust your spending next month. If you under-spend, put the extra money in your savings account or pay down a debt.

The benefit of having clutter-free money is a simpler life. Why does this matter? Not only will you be less consumed by managing your everyday money, you will be prepared to manage any unexpected life event that comes your way because your bills get paid on time, you know what accounts you have, and your spending is managed. What if you suddenly become ill or something happens to your partner? Do you know where all your financial information is located? Your financial statements, credit cards, will etc.? Most women will tell you that once they have experienced a traumatic life event, such as the death of a spouse, they get their money house in order.

Finally, the benefit of having clutter-free money is it allows you to focus on goal-setting for your future. You will know exactly where you stand and how your money is directed.

Your Life Goals

Having a goal-centered approach in life will ensure you stay focused on what matters. It will also help you manage your money better, because you will think twice about spending it on "stuff", instead of saving toward a goal. Balance your work goals with your life goals for more success. Remember that life goals can include giving back to the community. Giving to others is a great way to feel better about yourself and the world around you.

There has been a powerful shift in ideals and values from the "prosperity of the body" to the "prosperity of the soul." As people age, they tend to give more of themselves outwardly and worry less about money. Bill Gates spent decades building the Microsoft Empire, but now distributes much of his wealth to people in need, through the Bill Gates Foundation which fights disease and improves education. Great people are remembered less for the millions they made, than for their service to humanity which reflects a prosperity of the soul.

A lifelong passion can be triggered by an epiphany. For some it is the epiphany that life is not all about money. Doing something with your life that is highly meaningful and brings you satisfaction may be more powerful and more rewarding. It's time to dream big, realize your dreams, and to grab hold of life. It's time to start looking at the Big Picture.

Dorothy from the Wizard of Oz had an epiphany in the movie when she realizes "there is no place like home." She always had the power to get herself back home and the Good Witch knew this information, but did not share it with her. Dorothy had to learn to stand in her own strength and realize for herself that she had the power to get home. Sometimes happiness and our true passion can be staring us right in the face, but we are unable to see it, or don't know what to do with this desire. Why? Most of the time we are just not ready to see it. What is keeping you back from realizing your true potential or your ability to find happiness in your work and life?

As we prepare to start setting goals, now would be a great time to get out the vision board that you prepared, to help crystallize your thoughts and get more clarity on a vision for yourself and your future.

Goal Setting

A Savvy Money Gal lives by her goals.
Goal setting is at the heart of your future. If you want to achieve more, setting goals is the way to do it. It doesn't matter how much money you have or make. And as we discussed before, it doesn't matter if you are just starting out or have a successful career; setting goals will give you clarity. It will help you to stop squandering money and save more; it will help you become goal-oriented; and it will inspire you to open yourself up to new possibilities. It will connect you to your deepest desires and dreams.

There are many successful women out there who are living their lives as they want, living their Big Picture dreams. These are women working at what they love to do, and dedicated to working towards things they are passionate about. The more you love what you are doing, the harder you will work at it.

Do some soul searching and find your passion. Find out what motivates you. I have a great example to share, as there was a turning point in my life when I completed my MBA in 2010 at Western University, the Richard Ivey School of Business. For starters, there were only ten full-time women in my class of fifty-two students, making the total enrolment of women less than 25 %. I asked myself why? I could only surmise the answer: not every woman is able to go back to school, due to work-life commitments. Or, perhaps, when a woman is in a relationship this tends to limit her ability to strive for her personal goals, with or without kids. In my journey, I was able to afford this time for an MBA because of two key points: I created a financial plan to help me fund my degree and my partner stepped up and took on the lion's share of the home responsibilities and caring for our family. I would like to share a short story about the major life transition I made for myself. It gave me a great sense of purpose and was a challenging transitional journey.

Money Story: Anita

About five years ago, I reached a glass ceiling. I had a very good corporate job, but I felt something was holding me back from getting promoted. Prior to this time in my life, I thoroughly enjoyed my career and going into work every day. But my mood changed. I became negative and very self absorbed. Something was terribly wrong. I wasn't myself. I began to do some soul searching to figure out what was happening in my career and to find a way to overcome my barriers.

With some soul searching, I realized I needed a game changer, something big. I had always wanted to go to business school, but put this on hold to travel, get married, have a family etc. I had found excuses over the years not to pursue this higher education. Most of the time lack of money was the excuse I used. Unknowingly, I held myself back. I engaged my partner in conversation about our lives and our future, and he whole heartedly supported me going back to school and pursuing a business degree. He knew I needed a game changer. It was time to reignite my passion for learning and to go back to school. I enrolled in an eighteen month executive MBA at Western University, the Richard Ivey School of Business. I didn't let money hold me back and found ways to fund my education through financial planning. We will talk more about the benefits of financial planning later.

I spent the eighteen months of my degree still working part-time, caring for my family and trying to balance a major shift in my time. I had school obligations that took priority; some months required that I spend days away from home. My partner took over many home responsibilities. Together we successfully managed this life transition. It was a major life change to become a student once again in my forties! But with a goal in place, with my calendar as my best friend, I was on purpose. My family was on my calendar and I did what I had to do. It was often a struggle to do group work away from home, when all I wanted was to be at home. This is how I lived my life: one month at a time, with my eighteen month goal in mind. I balanced and juggled, every day and every week. I was fully dedicated toward achieving my MBA. I was living out my dream. I am proud to say that graduating with my degree in 2010 was one of the best things I ever did in my life. And through this journey, my life changed.

After I graduated, I found I had outgrown so much of my old world. I found adapting extremely difficult. With my new found knowledge and accomplishment in achieving an MBA, I was inspired. I felt ready to smash the glass ceiling in my life. I was inspired to start my own company and to write about my journey. Most of all, I wanted to use what I learned working in the corporate world of finance to help women improve their lives.

A Savvy Money Gal is never too old to learn something new.

Ask yourself this question: "if I had a million dollars in the bank, what kind of work would I be doing? Would I leave my job and move on to something really exciting, something that I have always wanted to do?" If so, then ask yourself – "Why am I not doing this right now? What is holding me back? Am I holding myself back? Am I letting a lack of available money or savings holding me back? Have I come to a place in life where I feel stuck?" You need to start thinking about what inspires, engages, and interests you today. You must not let money or your own thinking hold you back.

A Savvy Money Gal manages her future.

I believe we are in control of our lives and have the ability to orchestrate and achieve our goals with a winning mindset and hard work. Often women's biggest barrier is something being out of their direct control. Interestingly, a lack of money is often cited as a barrier for not moving forward. This obstacle can be overcome. Sometimes in order to unleash your true passion, changing your job is the first step. It is really easy to get stuck with the same old, same old, and stay in a job way too long. Why? It is often because you are comfortable, comfortable with the security of something you know. Many people will compromise themselves by staying in jobs they don't like, because they know what to expect and the pay is good. This is a routine behaviour. Don't let this be you. It can drain you of energy and spirit, leaving you miserable. Your job may provide your livelihood today, but it does not need to determine your future nor your stepping stones to your future.

Money Story: Sarah

Sarah gave up everything to pursue her passion of teaching literacy to children in Africa. She quit her job, withdrew some money from her retirement savings, and went abroad to help children in need. Sarah didn't realize how empty she was, until she started following her passion and making a difference in the lives of children who had relatively nothing. She doesn't make much money today, but she defines herself as being a richer woman. And most of all, Sarah is happy.

Sarah is an interesting example, because many of us would secretly like to quit our jobs. Each of us has had the dream of walking into the office one morning and telling our manager we are quitting. Sarah's choices may seem drastic to many of you. You may secretly wish to do what she did, but have no idea how you would make ends meet, pay bills, and live comfortably. Many of Sarah's friends still don't understand how she walked away from "everything." But Sarah made a life-altering change in her life to get to where she wanted to go. By all accounts, Sarah is happier than ever before. Imagine her strength to be able to listen to her heart. It can take courage to exercise your goals but life can be more meaningful as a result.

Creating Your Big Picture

We have spent some time engaging in a journey of self-discovery. Your tool kit is full of practical strategies and tools to create a new path for yourself. As we reinvent ourselves, we enter into a very exciting time of mapping out our future. You are ready to start defining goals or perhaps changing or augmenting ones you may already have. Get ready because your emotional well-being will take a giant leap forward as you tackle the biggest piece of the puzzle – your Big Picture goals.

Regardless of what goals or dreams you select for yourself, it is important that you approach them mindfully. What I mean by this is that you have to keep looking at where you are in life and evaluate whether what you are pursuing is fulfilling you and creating a life of meaning that aligns with your value system. Clearly, the other important element to goal setting and dream-making is your value system. Let's circle back to your values and keep them front and centre for this part of the book. Pursuing a goal or dream that is congruent with your values is a recipe for happiness. Values keep you grounded and focused on what matters.

Goals can provide us with many benefits. They can provide financial, emotional, and spiritual benefits. When we are younger, many of our goals are for getting ahead or getting more established. However, as we get older, our finances can become less important and more personally directed towards giving back.

A Savvy Money Gal balances short and long-term goals.

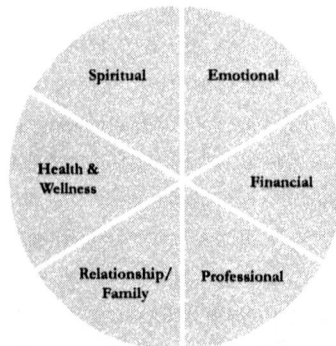

A Savvy Money Gal is very present in her life and consciously aware. She is mindful of how she spends her time. Her goals are a beacon guide for her future. It must be a purposeful journey. When you think about goals, think about two time periods: short and long-term. A short-term goal is something you want to accomplish in a short period of time, in no longer than a 3-5 year period; while a longer term goal will take longer time, more than 5 years. A short term goal might be wanting to save money to purchase a home, whereas a long-term goal might be to pay off your mortgage. Goals need to be categorized into short- and long-term. Many goals come with stepping stones. For example, if your goal is to attend college or university, you may first need to finish high school. This is a basic example to provide clarity around goal setting.

There are generally six broad categories of goals: professional, health and wellness, spiritual, financial, emotional, and relational. An emotional goal could be something like "becoming more positive" or "becoming less fearful in life." A financial goal could be something like "saving a particular amount of money." A professional goal could be something like "finding a new job" or "getting a promotion." A relationship or family goal could be something like "starting a family" or "finding a life partner." A health and wellness goal could be something like "losing ten pounds" or "consuming less coffee or red wine." And finally, a spiritual goal could be something like "going to church more often." Each one of us will have different goals, because we are at different stages of our lives.

6 Major Goal Categories

A Savvy Money Gal prioritizes her goals.

You need to attach yourself to your goals. You own them – the creation, the journey, and the outcomes. By attaching yourself to them, you become accountable.

When you pursue a dream for the sole purpose of an economic gain or money grab, you lessen its value. Some people choose a goal based on the need to support their ego. For example, seeking fame provides only fleeting satisfaction. When you completely attach yourself and submit yourself to a goal, the satisfaction lasts longer. Ask yourself a simple question: "is my soul in this goal?" If the answer is yes, you have alignment. If the answer is no, you may wish to re-evaluate it.

When you operate from a field of awareness of where you want to go, you have the ability to choose your course of action and manage your money better. You may have been thinking for some time of changes you want to make. You need to be fully engaged to your future goal and your desire to change, to get you to where you want to go. When you announce your goals to the world, you are actually committing to creating the change you want. Be careful of announcing your goals however. Remember that as you grow and change you may be upsetting the apple cart and those around you. Some people might want to sabotage your aspirations; your goals might not fit their image of you and might make them feel uncomfortable. Don't expect your friends or even your partner to embrace the changes you want to make in your life immediately- they like the old you and they might be uncomfortable with who you want to become. They may be uncertain as to how they will fit into your changed life.

Confidence Booster When planning your retirement, create a plan that will give you meaning, joy, and purpose. This will boost your emotional well-being.

Motivation is important, but maintaining a winning mindset is essential. When you commit your heart to your dream, you will create the energy around yourself to propel you forward. You will also have to expand your energy around your money. By this I mean the notion of redirection. The more you redirect your money toward your goals the more you will empower yourself to achieve them.

Here is a Savvy Money Gal tip on goal setting. Creating a personal goal for yourself is about creating a life that is important and meaningful to you. It's your Big Picture, the vision that you define and that you own. You probably are recreating and redefining what matters to you all the time and that is fine.

Who you are today on your journey is your starting point. It is where you begin to create your Big Picture. It will take time, but the outcome will provide you with confidence, clarity and control. You will boost your emotional well-being because you are creating the life you want and deserve.

Retirement Goals for the Sixty-Plus Gal

If you are like many women today, the thought of retirement planning might seem far away as you struggle day-to-day to manage your family and finances. But for boomers, retirement is just around the corner or has arrived. The good news is that research tells us that many women are looking forward to retirement. Given that women are living longer, many of us could possibly spend over one third of our lives in retirement. The bad news, according to retirement planning expert Moshe Milevsky, is that women will need 21% more money than men in retirement for a whole array of reasons.

Money aside, most women haven't given any thought to what they will need, where they will live, or what they will do during their retirement years. If you are like most women in their late fifties and early sixties, you are probably starting to wonder if you have saved enough to retire or if you will have to continue working. For women in their late sixties, lifestyle is top of mind.

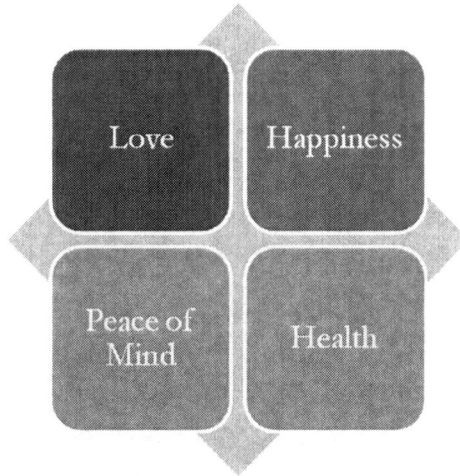

Exercise: Creating Your Big Picture

Let's have some fun now and create the Big Picture of your future! Recall that we did some exercises around creating your vision board earlier. Now might be a good time to get your vision board out and to align it with the following exercises.

Where am I today?

Find a quiet spot, light a candle, put on some peaceful music, close your eyes, and think about your life. What is most important to you? What and whom are you grateful for? How did you get here and is this the path you want to continue on? This is your story – lived by you.

It may be the first few chapters of your life or it could be a novel. It doesn't matter. Take some time now to reflect on the following: love, happiness, health, and peace of mind.

The Four Cornerstones of Your Life

Love

How are you feeling about love? What's right in your life? Is your heart open? Is it closed? Why?

_____

_____

_____

Health

How is your health? Are you taking care of yourself? What are you concerned about? Is anything bothering you?

_____

_____

_____

Peace of Mind

How do you feel overall? Do you have a sense of purpose and meaning in your life? What creates feelings of "peace of mind?" Are you connected to those who matter to you? Are you growing? If so, how? If not, why not? If you had all the money in the world, would you change your life? If yes, why and how? If no, why not?

_____

_____

_____

Happiness

How do you define happiness? How happy are you today with your life and where it is going? Do you indulge in simple pleasure or luxuries? Do you look at happiness differently now? What is driving this change in you?

_____

_____

_____

Creating My Big Picture

You have spent some time reflecting on your life and your four cornerstones – love, happiness, health, and peace of mind. We are going to really stretch your thinking now!

My Home

Think about where you are living today – your surroundings. Why are you living here? Is it close to work or family? Do you like where you live? What would you change? How well does your home suit your life right now? Have you outgrown it? Think about your future. Where do you want to live and why? How close will your friends and family be? How important is that to you? How do you feel about living alone now or in the future?

_____

_____

_____

My Personal Space

Think about your home and your personal space. Is it working? Are you happy in your space? If yes, what is it about your space that you love? What, if anything, do you want to change? What does your space mean to you? Do you feel safe? Is your space an oasis of calm or of chaos? If it's chaos, how do you change that? And with whom do you have to negotiate to make that happen?

_____

_____

_____

My Working Life

Think about your work life in terms of phases in your life. What are your primary goals for working? How do you feel about where you are in your work life? What would you change? What needs to happen to make that change a reality? Do you have your dream job? What is your dream job?

_____

_____

_____

My Family

Your family life is dynamic and ever-changing. How important is your family in your everyday life? Who are you including in this? Is there anything going on in your family now that could keep you from fulfilling your Big Picture goals? Have you created a wall around yourself to keep past family hurt away? What would you change in your current family situation? Who could you reach out to for help in making the change?

_____

_____

_____

My Personal Wellness

Think about your personal wellness on many levels – physical, emotional, and spiritual. How are you feeling overall? How are you doing today? Do you feel good? What changes do you need to make to be healthier emotionally, spiritually, and physically? What are you doing today that is really working? What would you like to be doing? What small steps could you take to get there?

_____

_____

_____

My Education

Think about education in the context of lifelong learning. Most of us learn new things every day from reading, taking courses, and just talking to people. What gaps do you have in your education? Do you want to go back to school to finish a program you left due to other priorities? What education do you need to get to the next level? Do you really need more education or would a mentor help you grow? What would you like to be doing? What small steps could you take to get there?

_____

_____

_____

My Community

Women are always volunteering, helping somebody, bonding, and supporting. Are you using your volunteer time well? Is this the right time in your life to be doing this? Are you using your skills in the best way possible? Is there an organization that you would like to volunteer with? Why is this organization important to you? Is there a way in which you can give back that works with your schedule and responsibilities? How can you go about accomplishing this? What are the best ways for you to use your time?

_____

_____

_____

My Personal Legacy

Many people think about a personal legacy in terms of how they want to be remembered when they are gone. How are you celebrating your life today? What does it mean to you to create a personal legacy?

What could you be doing to start creating a legacy for yourself? What can you do today to get you closer towards achieving your legacy?

_____

_____

_____

Outlining Your Goals

It is a challenge to think about the life we really want. It is easier to think about what we don't like or want. We spent some time going through a series of thought provoking questions. You asked yourself some very important questions about what creates meaning for you, and what makes you happy. You might have shared some of your ideas with those closest to you and I hope you were encouraged to set your goals high and follow your dreams.

Now that you have a better idea about where you want to go, let's begin by narrowing your goals to your top three priorities. By choosing just three priorities, you will be able to focus and set yourself up to win. Taking on too much is never wise and besides, you have a busy life. Let's do one thing at a time – or three!

Enter a description of your first goal under the heading The Savvy Money Gal Big Picture Goal #1 on the next page, do the same for your second and third goals under The Savvy Money Gal Big Picture Goal #2 and The Savvy Money Gal Big Picture Goal #3 headings. Recall that generally there are six types of goals: spiritual, emotional, financial, professional, relationship/family, and health and wellness. Do your best to identify which category your goals belong to. This will help you to see the bigger picture for yourself and which areas of your life are your major priorities.

The Savvy Money Gal Big Picture Life Goal #1 (Be specific)

What is my timeline? (Be time specific)

_____

_____

_____

What are the key steps I need to take?

_____

_____

_____

What will it cost?

_____

_____

_____

Who should I talk to in order to help me achieve my goal?

_____

_____

_____

How will I stay on track and not lose sight of this goal?

_____

_____

_____

The Savvy Money Gal Big Picture Life Goal #2 (Be specific)

What is my timeline? (Be time specific)

_____

_____

_____

What are the key steps I need to take?

_____

_____

_____

What will it cost?

_____

_____

_____

Who should I talk to in order to help me achieve my goal?

_____

_____

_____

How will I stay on track and not lose sight of this goal?

_____

_____

_____

The Savvy Money Gal Big Picture Life Goal #3 (Be specific)

What is my timeline? (Be time specific)

_____

_____

_____

What are the key steps I need to take?

_____

_____

_____

What will it cost?

_____

_____

_____

Who should I talk to in order to help me achieve my goal?

_____

_____

_____

How will I stay on track and not lose sight of this goal?

_____

_____

_____

You will want to refer to your vision board often to keep you grounded and focused on your goals. Celebrate your mini-milestones along the way. If your goal is to save $40,000 for a major purchase such as the down payment of a new home, and you reach a goal of saving $10,000, celebrate this success. Remember goals are meant to be beacons or sign posts for our journey in life. Things can happen that might change your goals. You may achieve your goals faster than you expected or you may change your goals with new found priorities. The point is that setting goals is a sure fire way to keep you focused on what matters and to make sure your money is directed in a way that will bring you happiness.

Connecting with You

1. Do you feel there is anything holding you back from reaching the goals you set for yourself?

2. How do you feel your life will evolve and unfold as a result of setting and achieving your new goals?

3. Did you learn anything new about yourself that you didn't know before? Did you see yourself at all in my story of recreating myself by following my goal?

4. How is your journal writing progressing? What surprised you in your entries? You might have seen a major shift in the content of your money diary. I suspect that your thoughts have become much more soulful and real. I also suspect that you are thinking less about the past. Your entries are most definitely more positive and you may feel that now might be a good time to reduce how often you write. I leave it up to you. You may also have found a wonderful new outlet to express your thoughts. It might be the beginning of a book!

Chapter Six ~ Strategy #6
Rely on Yourself for Your Financial Security

"I, with a deeper instinct, choose a man who compels my strength, who makes enormous demands on me, who does not doubt my courage, or my toughness, who does not believe me naïve or innocent, who has the courage to treat me like a woman."
Anais Nin (1903-1977) French Writer and Diarist

Personal Learning Goal

As you read through this chapter, the last of the 6 Savvy Money Gal Strategies, you will be introduced to one of the most powerful life-changing strategies. Our personal learning goal in this chapter is to learn the skills to stand in your own strength, and the empowerment you will get from relying on yourself for your financial future and security. You will learn strategies to find more balance of power in a partner relationship, to get your money to work for you today, and to learn about the power of investing. I will teach you how to kick start your savings as a precursor to investing. You will discover the six go-to financial experts you need in your life to help you become more financially successful and secure. And finally, the moment of truth arrives when you take your Big Picture goals and engage in conversations with either a financial planner or an investment advisor. They will take your life goals and make them very real for you.

This chapter builds on the previous five. In the last chapter, you probably had the most fun on our journey together, by creating the Big Picture goal you have for yourself and your future. Pin it beside your vision board. Keep a copy of it with you. By creating your Big Picture, you have made a conscious choice to harness your energies and direct your future. As you move forward, you will engage in conscious choice and mindful spending, because you know your goals are what matter to you. Your life is clutter-free and thus you will continue to spend your money in a disciplined, streamlined, focused manner that will propel you toward your goals. A clutter-free life results in a mindful, self-disciplined woman on the road to increased financial security —living with increased happiness, energy, and power as she stands in her own strength.

Men, Love, and Money

When men enter our lives, we women often put our lives on hold to help support and further our partner's career and to rear children. Kathleen Cox, a leading Clinical Psychologist, has conducted extensive research on women and money. She is amazed to see how women change when they enter into relationships. She was quoted as saying, "I see a lot of previously ambitious women who are very confused by a sudden urge to bake cakes and sew curtains, which totally flies in the face of everything they strived for. They begin to wonder 'who am I?' Because they don't recognize themselves anymore."

Many women today still follow old family values, ideals, and cultural mythologies about men, women and marriage. Women today are more independent, marrying later and engaging in major financial decisions well in advance of marriage. Twenty-eight is the average age of marriage for women today. Yet even today, how many women are comfortable making decisions for themselves or putting themselves first? Most women will put their partner and children first. Until this situation changes, we are still working with old paradigms and values.

> *"Most women are one man away from welfare."*
> **Gloria Steinem (1934-) Feminist and Activist**

Romantic relationships can be rich and fulfilling, and bring tremendous emotional well-being for women. When women balance the power in their relationships, they empower themselves and their children. Traditional relationships can prove tricky for some women to navigate. In reality, raising the next generation is probably one of the most important yet undervalued jobs. No one gets paid for raising their children. Whichever partner stays at home to raise the children relies on their partner's financial support. In the case of women, this might erode their sense of self worth. In the past, women were proud to be homemakers. Nowadays, there are fewer and fewer stay-at-home moms.

A Savvy Money Gal stands in her own strength.

There are fundamental differences between how men and women view and manage money. Men are generally more engaged and more literate around money. Men are greater risk takers and typically stay better informed. To this end, relationships can often become imbalanced around money. And when there is an imbalance in a relationship, usually power shifts to the stronger of the two in the relationship. This explains why money is the number one reason partners fight and divorce.

Many women keep quiet when they get uncomfortable or they don't know something. Suffering in silence when you don't know something is not savvy. It is likely you are not a financial expert, but you don't need to be one to be successful in your life with money. In life, there are no dumb questions, only bad or ill informed choices. Sometimes, we let our lack of confidence and self-doubt keep us silent. We just accept what is presented to us or make choices that are uncomfortable, because we don't know any better.

A Savvy Money Gal has a healthy dose of respect for the men in her life.

No book about women and money is complete without discussing men. Is it? You can't read an article today or search the web without finding something to remind you that being with a man is not an insurance policy or a financial plan. Each and every woman must stand in her own strength because when we do, our relationship with the men in our lives changes from economic helplessness or dependence, to one of economic empowerment. When we balance the power in our relationships, we demonstrate how we can stand in our own strength and abandon a perceived lack of ability to be self-sufficient. The men in our lives can include our fathers, grandfathers, husbands, boyfriends, brothers, sons, and grandsons.

A Savvy Money Gal engages in interdependent relationships.

In order to reach your goals, you must stand in your own emotional and economic strength. There is no reason why you can't. Relying on others for your financial security is risky. It is not self-empowering and will not help you to increase the financial security you seek. This chapter will give you some strategies and show you how to stand in your own financial strength and abandon economic helplessness. It will give you more tools and access to people who are trained to help you invest your money and get more out of life. When we relinquish control of our financial future, we can engage in activities that will hinder our financial security. Many successful women I know are fully reliant on their partners for their financial and emotional strength. While I believe in financial interdependency between partners, I do not support the relinquishing of any woman's future to someone or something else.

> *"Marry for love because you can make your own money!"*
> **Anonymous**

Sadly, 50% of marriages end in divorce. Research tells us that one in five women fall into poverty as a result of divorce. One in four divorced mothers doesn't receive child support. These statistics reflect key findings from the Canadian Women's Foundation. If you are in a bad marriage or partnership at the moment and you are feeling uncertain about your future, you must start preparing yourself by creating a transition plan. If marriage counselling doesn't work or isn't an option, divorce may be inevitable. This is not to instil fear or to be pessimistic. You need to be prepared and not caught off guard. This is reality.

Money Story: June

Some men can be money bullies using money for power and control, which in turn harms and intimidates women. A money bully will keep you where they want you, which is typically economic helplessness. The solution is to create your own financial success and push back; don't let them bully you. Dealing with a money bully is not easy. We have already touched on the power of money and how money can create an imbalance in partnerships. A "Merrill Lynch 2013 survey reports that well over half of married couples (57 %) have arguments over money." The survey cites money disputes as a significant contributor to almost one in three divorces.

Men have a history of using money in relationships to create personal power. They might use money to shift the balance of power in a relationship and seek dominance, resulting in a decrease in their female partner's self-confidence and personal worth. Why do you think so many rich women are in therapy?

> *"Heed the still, small voice that so seldom leads us wrong, and never into folly."*
> **Madame du Deffand (1697-1780)**
> **Marquise du Deffand/Patron of the Arts**

Financial Interdependency

There is nothing wrong with engaging in a healthy dose of financial interdependency in romantic relationships. In fact, interdependency is a sign of a healthy relationship. It can harness great power and financial results; the economic power of two income earners is better than one.

Most people combine their money surveys show. Marriage therapist Beth Erickson says when couples pool their finances "greater intimacy results." Her view is shared by many Americans, and Merrill Lynch's Affluent Insights Survey in February 2013 reported that 89% of married couples manage their money collaboratively.

Independence has been coveted by many for a long time been. Women are told to become completely independent with regards to their life and money. But is this really what is best for women and society? Being independent is an old paradigm and one used to scare women into thinking that they have to be strong and live independently. Women must be able to stand in their own strength, but they can also stand strong in a relationship with a partner where there is economic interdependency. There isn't anyone in this world who is completely independent. So why do we keep telling women they need to be independent? Why don't we tell women and men to engage in money interdependency? I know this, because I do. When you share in a partnership, you share the good, the bad, and the ugly. A couple who shares together stays together.

When women enter into an emotional relationship with a man, this should not be confused with a financial relationship. I am a happily married woman; however, before I met my husband, I was independent. Throughout our lives together there have been moments where each of us has relied on the other, not only for emotional strength, but also for financial strength. In most partner relationships, there are times where one partner can be out of work while the other carries the burden for the family. This is interdependency between couples. When you are completely dependent on someone else for your emotional and financial security you relinquish control and become vulnerable. The best relationships are ones in which you can rely on someone and they can rely on you. To create partnerships where the balance of power is equal, women must approach relationships with equal footing.

> *"No man is an island, entire of it; every man is a piece of the continent, a part of the main."*
> **John Donne, No Man Is An Island (1572-1631) Poet**

Why Investing Matters

A Savvy Money Gal invests in her future.

One of the best ways to learn to stand in your own economic strength is to invest your money. Investing can create anxiety for people, especially for women who may not be educated about it, and don't really understand what investing entails. And if you have had a bad experience and lost money, there is no doubt in my mind you are probably afraid of investing and losing your money again. Be aware of your anxiety and share it with a friend or partner.

> *"Never depend on a single income. Make investment to create a second source."*
> **Warren Buffett (1930-) CEO**

Learning the basics of investing is a must. You don't have to become an expert but you owe it to yourself to understand how investing works and why it matters. At the back of the book, I have included a list of key investment terms to get you started and more familiar with investing. The concepts will familiarize you with the terms financial professionals use in conversations about money. Thus, you will have an idea of what is being discussed and can engage in deeper and richer conversations with confidence. There are many websites that offer free online resources about investing, examples are TD Waterhouse (Canadian website: www.tdwaterhouse.com) and Fidelity Investments (US website: www.fidelity.com). These sites offer easy to use resources and materials to learn more about investing.

Research tells us that women avoid investing. Many women feel that investing is complicated. It can be, but it doesn't have to be that way for you. Watching the news might make you feel that investing is only for people who have a lot of money and for those who understand the stock and bond markets. Before we go any further find out how you feel about investing, because once you understand yourself better, you can make more informed decisions. Answer the following questions:

1. How confident do you feel about investing?

_____

_____

2. What if anything is holding you back from investing your money?

_____

_____

3. Have you ever experienced financial losses as a result of investing your money?

_____

_____

4. What is your biggest fear about investing?

_____

_____

5. What qualities do you need to show to overcome your fear?

_____

_____

The statistics vary in terms of how many women are investing their money beyond having a savings account. I plan to broaden your perspective on what might be holding you back from investing your money.

Money Story: Anita

I would like to share another installment of my money story to demonstrate the importance of investing for your future financial security. My early experiences with investing were positive and set the tone for twenty years of self-directed investing. I was twenty-two when I started investing in the stock market. I took the Canadian Securities course and made it a priority to learn about investing. My mom encouraged me to invest in solid blue-chip companies. She explained that owning a piece of a company through common shares is savvy and, in the long run, would increase my financial security. I listened and she was right. She had given me a quick overview of the power of the markets. I was hooked.

I made a plan. I started small. With each paycheque I would set money aside for my savings. I also got a piece of advice that has helped me tremendously: stick with what you know; which for me meant investing in the stocks of the company I was working for. Not only was my employer a solid blue-chip company, but they had a stock purchase program through which they would match contributions and provide the flexibility to make additional cash contributions. My foray into investing resulted in a positive outcome and set the tone for my ongoing interest in it.

My goals were clear. I wanted to buy a home on my own and kick start my retirement savings. I did both. In order to accelerate reaching my goal, I took on a part-time job, working on the odd evenings and weekends. I wanted to move on to the next phase of my life.

> *"Investors, as human beings, find it hard to balance what may be optimal long term decisions against different decisions that are made in the short term to reduce anxiety."*
> **Barclays Wealth & Investment Management 2013**

Investing is the best way to build your personal wealth. It can help you create a financial cushion for yourself, so you can stop worrying about money or not having enough of it. You can start investing at any time, even with the smallest amount of money. Given that women are living longer, we want to make sure we don't run out of money in our golden years. Investing is a long-term approach to managing your money and one that requires you to stay the course and ride the ups and downs. Many people, when faced with a potential loss of money, will panic and act in ways that are short-term focused in order to ease the fear. Most forms of investing, such as investments in stocks (equities) or bonds, have some form of risk. There are, however, ways to manage investment risk. Investing has more risk than putting money into a savings account, but it also has the potential to make more money than a savings account could yield. Investing your money is a process that goes beyond just saving money in a bank account. It's a start.

Many women feel that having a savings account or a retirement savings account is investing. It really isn't. Investing means putting money into the stock or bond market, exchange traded funds

(ETFs) or into a mutual fund, and getting it to work for you beyond what you could earn in a savings account. Investing also includes real estate, private equity investing etc. Many people have made a lot of money in real estate, but the focus of our discussion will be around the stock market. Depending on where you are in your life, you might not have the time to become an expert in investing and so will need to rely on good, expert advice to help you achieve your financial goals. It is a fact that because women more often than not have less financial resources at their disposal, they tend to be more risk adverse. This is particularly true of women who are living in retirement today.

Your lack of understanding or knowledge, and the lack of trust in financial markets may play an important role in curbing your participation. It is difficult to know who to trust, particularly with your money. Short-term thinking can hurt you in the long-term. Many people get hung up on past performance of investments as the benchmark or indicator of future success. Past performance tells us a story of what happened in the past; it doesn't predict the future. Getting concerned about rates-of-returns over the years, can create undue worry and stress. The most important part of investing is managing yourself and your behavior. You will need to find a trusted financial advisor or planner to help you achieve your life goals.

> **Confidence Booster**
> Staying on the sidelines is safe, but it can create a glass ceiling for you and hold you back. Jump in!

"Investors, as human beings, find it hard to balance what may be optimal long term decisions against different decisions that are made in the short term to reduce anxiety." Barclays Wealth & Investment Management 2013

The steps to investing are simple: first and foremost you must embrace a winning mindset around investing; stick with what you know; don't overlook the company that employs you as an investment opportunity; find a good mentor or someone whose investment philosophy and approach resonates with you; start small; manage risk; diversify; and most importantly engage professionals for advice.

Over or Under Confidence with Money

Leading experts in Behaviour Economics and Finance have identified overconfidence as an emotion that can cause a lot of investment errors. An overconfident investor might easily get involved in Ponzi schemes or financial frauds. Some of you may know the story of Bernie Madoff, the former stockbroker and investment advisor in the United States who preyed on innocent victims and bilked them of their savings. Many of the people he worked with were vulnerable, such as older women living alone who had accumulated a lot of wealth from their husbands.

Many of these women are now working, because they have no money left in their retirement funds. Because they have little time to recover their investment, they are forced to work. Investing in a get-rich-quick scheme comes from putting far too much faith in an individual around investments. In life, having healthy skepticism is a good thing.

If you are overconfident and not grounded about your future and your ability to make money, you may set yourself up for failure. For example, many entrepreneurs are overly idealistic but not realistic about their future, and this can run them into trouble if they don't manage their cash flow, sales pipeline, and expenses well.

If you are under-confident about your money and investing, you are engaging in economic helplessness and are directly contributing to your lack of financial success. You are effectively creating a glass ceiling for yourself based on your choice not to invest. Being under-confident can cause just as much hardship as being overconfident. When we don't have enough confidence to take action, we risk staying on the sidelines and missing out on engaging in investing and finding more economic and financial security.

Risk and Safety of Money

The reality is that the older we get, the more fearful we become with numbers. For many of us, we understand basics terms, but it is the more complicated terms that often hold us back from investing. We create a perceived inability to invest; we self-sabotage.

Your Life Goals Add Up

The cost of life goals can be daunting. Recent research in the US shows that the cost of life goals for an average person can be over $1.5 million dollars. According to the US Census Bureau, in order to retire comfortably, women will need a nest egg of approximately $750,000, which will provide 60% of 2012's median household income of $60,000. You may be thinking that $1.5 million is a lot of money. It is. You may be wondering how on earth you are ever going to afford all your goals. Well, if you don't invest your money, you reduce your chances. And remember, a man is not a financial plan and waiting for an inheritance or windfall creates economic helplessness and relinquishes control over your life. In Citibank's Citi Blog's article "Putting a Price Tag on Life's Financial Goals" by Jonathan Clements, the approximate cost of different life goals are listed:

Cost of life goals:

Retirement: $750,000 (US Census Bureau)
Home ownership: $280,000 + (US Department of Housing and Urban Development)
Raising a family: $300,000 up to age 17/18 (US Department of Agriculture)
Cost of college/university: $71,000 for four years (College Board United States)
Long-term care/nursing home: $87,000 in 2011 for an average private room per annum (MetLife Mature Market Institute)
Assisted living: $42,000 for an assisted living facility per annum (MetLife Mature Market Institute)

The figures suggest that life adds up for all of us. Raising a family may cost more or less than $300,000. It depends on how many children you have and the choices you make for them.

There are leading educators in the field of investing whom I encourage you to look at after you finish this book. Findependence Day is a book written by Jonathon Chevreau that seeks to demystify financial concepts by weaving them into the life journey of a young family. The book offers a step-by-step introduction to financial concepts based on the typical life cycle from starting out to retirement. Major concepts are introduced in a way that will not overwhelm you.

Build More Wealth Today

A Savvy Money Gal invests her money and gets it working for her.

Investing is just another way to build wealth and one that will, more often than not, accelerate the growth of your savings. Many of us dream of buying a home, paying off our mortgage, and travelling the world. Being able to visualize your future successes is essential for moving forward. We have already engaged in cognitive psychology, guided imagery, and visualization to create a mental path to where you want to go. We completed our exercises by identifying your goals and your Big Picture. When we are able to access our inner self, we are better able to direct ourselves and our actions towards fulfilling our goals. There are some distinct strategies you can follow to help you reach your goals sooner. Set up a consistent approach for yourself and stick to it.

A Savvy Money Gal finds joy in not spending money.

So how do you get started? First, embrace a winning attitude and become goal obsessed. Consciously start to look for joy in not spending money. Remember, we also discussed the value of "free", and that anything that is free is worth doing over and over again. Sometimes, we have to remind ourselves that we are not missing much in life and that what we have is probably enough. With a shift in your mindset, you will begin to really understand the power of saving money and will get really good at it. Be conscious of your spending. Remember that when we spend money, we engage in trade-offs. We trade-off one thing for something else. I would never tell you that you can't splurge or buy a new pair of shoes for $150. If this is something you want, I would never suggest denying yourself something you truly desire. How you direct your money is your decision. Realize you are making a trade-off against something else, such as saving for retirement, renovating your home, buying a new car. You get the picture.

A Savvy Money Gal finds joy in saving money.

Finding joy in saving money is the same as embracing a winning mindset around your money. These are core elements to future financial security. Saving money and having a spending plan are the most fundamental money management strategies. In my research on women and money, most women I know make an honest attempt to save money but many feel it is a burden that restricts their lifestyle. For most of us, saving is the most challenging money management strategy to enact. By shifting your mindset away from seeing saving as difficult to visualizing it as easy, you will start saving more money naturally.

If you want to save more money, the first step that you need to take is to shift your mindset away from thinking that saving money is a daunting and difficult task. Redirect your thinking more positively toward embracing a winning mindset around saving money.

Second, you may want to really explore your feelings about saving and why you may feel you can't save enough money, by writing about your feelings in your money journal. Dig deep and be honest with your feelings.

Third, circle back to the spending plan you created. With your spending plan and conscious-money decision making in place, you are using the tools to save more money and increase your financial security. By addressing your thought patterns and feelings, you will begin to see the obstacles that hold you back from saving more money.

Lastly, revisit your personal affirmation and add something about how much you love saving money! Remember, the framework we set at the beginning of this book can be tweaked to reflect your growth, new ideas, and new vision. You must take control over your thoughts and feelings about saving money. In Chapter Three, we discussed temporal discounting and instant gratification. Saving money is a long term strategy where the pay off comes much later. The sooner you start seeing saving money as a way to reach your goals, the sooner you will create a mental road map that will result in your success. Redirecting your thoughts about saving will set you on a path to reaching your goals sooner and living more comfortably.

A Savvy Money Gal pays herself first.

The best way I know how to start building more wealth and saving more money is to start small and make the process seamless or automatic. By this I mean that most major financial institutions offer pre-authorized payments or debit, a process to take money out of your account automatically and sweep it into a savings or investment account. You may already have a savings plan in place. This is terrific. If you don't, for every $100 you make, pay yourself $10 or 10%. Set it and forget it. Based on your spending plan and habits, you must be in a good position to know how much you really can save. Be smart about it. Make sure all your financial commitments and responsibilities are cared for. The sooner you start saving more money and making it a habit, and the more you accumulate, the faster you will be ready to invest, which is the next phase in building your financial wealth.

A Savvy Money Gal takes advantage of all her employee benefits.
Don't forget to look at your employee benefits, such as stock purchase plans or retirement savings programs. Often people overlook employee benefits that will automatically take money off of your pay and put it towards your savings. My research around employee benefits suggests that many people don't sign up because they think they will not be with their employer long and the paper work is cumbersome. Your employer, as my former employers did, might have a retirement or savings matching program where they will match a percentage of your contributions. This is "free" money and remember "free" is always best. Trust me, this is the best way to build more wealth, because you won't feel the pain of a slightly smaller paycheque.

Also, there could be other benefits offered, such as education assistance; special pricing on computers or other items; childcare support; and more standard benefits such as medical and dental coverage. There may be tax implications to the benefits but, nine times out of ten, the benefit will far outweigh the tax burden. And finally, most benefit plans allow you to make changes once a year or at the time of a major life event. This is important because you might not have to wait until the annual review process to make these changes.

When you move away from relying on others for your financial security, you take full control of your future life and you forge a road to financial success. You move from a state of economic helplessness to empowerment easily and naturally. You start to embrace interdependency and learn the benefits of having mutually beneficial relationships in your life. In fact, you might start to become a role model for others – your kids, friends, and maybe even your partner! You will no longer feel trapped in your life and you will stop engaging in economic helplessness. You will abandon the negative dogma that is present in the media and your skepticism will virtually vanish.

Six Must-Have Personal Finance Experts

A Savvy Money Gal has a circle of go-to financial experts at her fingertips.
Now is the time to breathe a huge sigh of relief. In your quest to become savvier with your money, realize that with a trusted circle of advisors you will position yourself for greater finan-

cial security. Most decisions we make have a financial impact or outcome. When you are savvy and consult with someone else about your financial decisions, you are leveraging their expertise to help you make informed decisions. Always remember that two heads are better than one and when you consult with others for their guidance, you ultimately own the decisions. It's your life. It's your money.

A Savvy Money Gal gets professional financial advice to save money and build wealth.
I work in the financial services industry and yet I still consult experts on a myriad of financial and investing questions. Then I make my decisions based on a careful analysis. Creating a circle of influence will empower you and lessen the burden you feel. You still might be thinking that you don't have enough money to hire or engage these financial professionals. But let me tell you something, you can't afford not to hire them in some capacity. Remember, you are not a financial expert. Your time is better spent taking care of yourself and family.

Life events put your money in motion. Each time you are faced with a life event, there are generally financial implications and choices to be made. There are definite life events when engaging a financial professional is essential to boost your emotional well-being. Recall from Chapter Two, the nine major life events: leaving home; becoming an official couple; building a family; suddenly single; sudden change in your money situation; change in career; starting a care giving journey; health concerns; and retirement. Each of these life events will result in financial transactions of some sort. Wouldn't you agree that if you had a circle of financial experts at your fingertips to help you manage the financial considerations, it would boost your emotional well-being and make you feel more in control of your life?

For example, should you be faced with a sudden change in your employment, you might need three to six months of emergency money to help you get through this. You may need to engage a financial planner to help you explore your options. Or, you may find yourself suddenly in a care giving role for a loved one. There are emotional and financial implications that accompany being a care giver. You might be required to take care of your parent's finances or help them to manage their money. Having a circle of experts you can turn to for help in navigating life's ups and downs is savvy.

Six Go-to Money Expert Categories

Accountant, Tax Specialist and/or Bookkeeper

An accountant is someone who helps you manage your financial resources by helping you complete and file your annual tax returns. These experts offer advice and guidance on how to get more money back on your tax return. They generally charge a flat fee for completing your taxes and will often be able to find deductions you are entitled to claim that you might not have found otherwise, thereby helping you save more money. If you run a small business, a bookkeeper will help you manage your cash flow, payables and receivables.

Family Lawyer, Divorce Lawyer

A family lawyer will work to protect your rights and best interests. They also work to help you obtain financial support such as alimony or spousal support. The documents they create are legal and binding in the jurisdiction in which they were created. They can also create a power of attorney for you, should something happen and you become disabled and unable to care for your own matters. A divorce lawyer will help you navigate through separation and divorce. It is prudent to know of one in the event you find yourself needing their services.

Life Coach

A life coach is someone who will help you further define your goals and show you how to overcome barriers that may be holding you back. Having already gone through the process of creating your goals, a life coach can help you stay on track, and manage any bumps or challenges.

Will and Estate Lawyer

An estate lawyer is a person or organization that will review your will and estate planning needs and objectives, providing you with specific advice based on your own personal situation. If you have children or assets, a will is necessary. If you don't have a will, these lawyers can help you draft one up, while advising you of the law. Estate lawyers offer advice and planning to ensure that your children and other beneficiaries are taken care of after you pass away. They also offer additional services in the context of wills and estates.

Mortgage Broker, Real Estate Agent, Real Estate Lawyer

When you are considering purchasing a home, you will need to engage professionals to complete the transaction: a mortgage broker, a real estate agent and a real estate lawyer. Each of these individuals plays a role in the transaction.

Confidence Booster
A financial plan will boost your emotional well-being and make you feel more in control of your future!

A mortgage broker does not work for a financial institution. They offer a service whereby they will negotiate with financial institutions to find you the best possible mortgage rates based on your qualifications. They are paid by financial institutions. You can go directly to your bank but most often the best deals come from mortgage brokers.

Real estate agents are trained to buy and sell property. They will help you find a property and will also help you to sell your home. As much as I would like to suggest that you save money and try to sell your home on your own, there are many benefits to engaging a real estate agent. Remember you are not an expert in real estate and therefore having someone work for you is the best solution. Trust me, you don't want to take on the headache of being your own agent.

Finally, a real estate lawyer will complete the legal documentation for the sale of your home or buying a new home. In most instances, you can get a discount on your lawyer's fees by having the same lawyer facilitate both ends of a deal, such as the purchase of a new home; and the sale of your existing home.

Financial Planner, Investment Advisor, Insurance Agent

Financial planners engage in the work of financial planning. They offer services to help you meet your financial goals. This includes investment planning, retirement planning, children's education planning, and major purchase planning such as for a new home, cottage, and other significant purchases. Planners will spend time learning about your goals. They will not spend time fleshing out your goals or going through all the key considerations of goal-planning that we discussed earlier in the book. They will focus instead on creating an investment objective for you based on your goals. They will also consider your risk tolerance and, based on your age and financial situation, recommend investments that are right for you. They also take into consideration inflation and taxes when drawing up a financial plan for you.

Some planners will also assist you with your borrowing needs or credit. This approach is holistic and many refer to this as "taking a full balance sheet approach." Put simply, a "full balance sheet" planner will look at your assets; investments, liabilities, loans, and mortgages. They will seek to optimize your financial position and are able to do so because they have a full picture of your money situation. They can also give you relevant advice on how to obtain a better credit rating or sustain a good one.

Many financial advisors have the ability and licenses to sell you the insurance you need. However, having a separate insurance agent might result in more specialized attention and service. You might find it more advantageous to separate your insurance from your investments and banking. Make sure that your financial planner is aware of the insurance services you already have.

Confidence Booster
You decide who you want to work with. Remember that people must earn your trust first. It's all about you. And not about them.

An insurance agent is a licensed professional who is able to sell you life, disability, and long-term care insurance. They are governed by various jurisdictions according to your province or state. They must follow general rules and meet compliance standards. Both life and disability insurance will protect you and your family should something happen to you. If you pass away suddenly, your family will be protected with a life insurance policy. Disability insurance helps you and your family cover expenses should you take ill and can't work. Insurance agents will advise you on the right amount of coverage that suits your need.

Trust Your Money

A Savvy Money Gal demands trust with her money.
When we think about trust there are two levels to examine. The first is trust we have with others, including third parties. The second is self-trust. Do you trust yourself enough to make the right decisions? Sometimes we are just not aware of our feelings and we don't make rational decisions. There have been times in my life when I have trusted someone only to find out they had a hidden agenda, an ulterior motive. It is hard to know who to trust at times.

Trust is at an all-time low. People do not trust each other, and many people do not trust organizations. Experts say that the 2008 financial crisis has eroded public confidence and trust in the United States government and financial system, however, the same was not found as much in Canada. Canadian banks are the exemplar of public confidence in banking. Yet, there is still cause for concern. Trust is the most essential component of any relationship, especially in managing your money! Trust can take many forms, because it includes trusting yourself to make the optimal decisions for yourself and your family. Trust also involves working with other people and letting them manage your money for you. Diluted trust makes it harder to manage your money.

If you are like most women, it is hard to trust others with your money. Managing your own money and that of your family's is a major responsibility. You guard your money very closely because you know its power. It can help you get the life you want for yourself and your family, and it can take care of you as you grow older. Many women have stories to share of lost financial trust. These stories are connected to feelings of pain, anguish and remorse. All of us at some point have said, "How could I have been so dumb with my money?" We enter into most financial situations with good intentions and seeking good outcomes.

Trust is one of the hardest things to build and the easiest to lose. Building trust in someone when your financial future is at stake is a process that takes time. When engaging in conversation with people about your money, you are wise to enter the relationship slowly, and gradually reveal personal and pertinent information about yourself. I will share some tips of how to find an advisor you can trust. Referrals from friends are often the best way to find somebody.

When you commence working with anyone new, particularly a financial services professional, there are three things they need to demonstrate: credibility, reliability, and empathy. The biggest challenge you will face is coming to terms with the fact that all financial advisors are in business to make money from you. Many people think that their advisor is working for them, when in essence they are working for themselves. The trick is to find someone whose self-interest doesn't trump your needs. Let's spend some time discussing trust.

When I worked at BMO Bank of Montreal we trained advisors on two levels: 1) how to engage in conversations with their clients and 2) how to become trusted advisors. In 2011, we worked with Blue Rush Media to develop a skills based learning program which received the 2011 award for being the Best Online Banking video from the Internet Marketing Association. What I found was that the advisors and planners who took the training seriously were completely dedicated to building a practice where they could build deep trust with their clients. Trust, though, can work on many different levels. For some of us, we don't trust ourselves with our money and we don't trust others with our money either.

Ask yourself these important questions on trust:

- Do I trust myself with my money?
- Do I trust others with my money?
- Do I trust my partner with money and making money decisions that will impact my future?

Answering these questions may initially appear straightforward but for some of you it may be more challenging. Why? It goes back to the betrayal of trust or past money mistakes. The only way to leave the past behind and truly move forward when trust has been breached is to forgive and to move forward as a wiser person.

When your financial future is at stake, there are things you can do to increase your level of trust with others. Women have a wonderful thing called "intuition." My friend Barb refers to this as her "spidey sense", a term taken from the comic book Spiderman. How many of us ignore our "spidey sense", discounting and ignoring it. In most instances, your internal radar, your feelings of discomfort, are probably right. If something doesn't feel right to you, don't do it, or seek more clarity.

Tips to Find a Trustworthy Financial Professional

Finding someone to work with you can be a daunting task. You may not know where to start. Here are a few tips you might want to consider as you explore working with a new set of financial professionals. If you are already working with people, ask yourself one simple question: what have they done to show you they value your business?

Confidence Booster Create your own money circle of influence of go-to financial experts. You will boost your emotional well-being and never feel alone with your money.

Work with people you know.
Rely on referrals from friends and family. Ask for references. People must earn your business, so don't be afraid to interview several possible candidates before making your decision. Referrals are the greatest form of flattery and most people who get referred take referrals very seriously. Referrals result from doing a great job. Many businesses are built on referrals alone.

Seek expert advice.
If you had stomach problems, you would see a gastrointestinal doctor. This becomes tricky, particularly in the world of personal finance. When dealing with a financial services organization, there are so many different layers and people working for them that it is hard to discern who to talk to. To find the right person, always double check credentials to make sure you know who you are working with.

Know your needs.
Make sure you are focused and that the other person knows what you need. Use the technique of clarifying and confirming. Clarify that the other person understands your needs and confirm this by having them repeat your needs back to you. This will ensure there are no misunderstandings. Make sure you have everything in writing; if you don't, there are no guarantees.

Expect empathy and understanding.

Empathy builds understanding and trust. When engaging in conversation about your money, it is imperative that the other person shows empathy and understanding for you. If they don't, then this is probably not the right person for you. I often hear from women that they prefer to work with other women for the simple reason of requiring empathy.

Expect an open and flowing conversation.

Make sure your conversation is engaging, and that there is a two-way dialogue. If someone is using industry jargon or terms you don't understand, ask them not to use the jargon and to explain things more clearly. Some financial professionals will try to wow you with their understanding of the market. You don't want to be wowed. Most women are looking for simple answers to complex questions. Make sure the conversation feels open and transparent.

Fully understand the terms and conditions.

Read the fine print before signing anything. Remember, the devil is in the details. If you don't understand something, take time to reflect. Schedule another appointment. Never feel pressured.

Financial Planning for your Future!

You will boost your emotional well-being, feel more in control of your future, and reach your goals sooner with a financial plan. Many women don't really understand the concept of financial planning, what it is; how they will benefit from it; who it is for; and how to go about developing a financial plan. Many people have the misconception that financial planning is only for people with a lot of money. This is not true. I prefer fee-based financial planners because they will create a financial plan for you regardless of how much money you have. There are many fee-only financial planners in North America.

Financial planning is a disciplined approach to money management and will put you on the right path to achieving your goals. It will increase your control and confidence over your money. Like a spending plan, it is a process that requires some endurance. Financial planning is a long-term approach to money management.

Most financial plans are ten pages in length, connecting your life goals to your money. Having 401K or an investment account is not a financial plan. Having a Registered Retirement Savings Plan (RRSP), Registered Education Savings Plan (RESP) or a brokerage account of self-directed investments is not a financial plan. A financial plan is typically a ten page document outlining your major life goals and a plan to get you there through sections on major purchases, education and retirement. People who engage in financial planning are more likely to feel in control of their money and boost their emotional well-being.

Statistics vary, but the VIP Forum, a leading research organization in the US, indicates that less than 60% of people created or updated their financial plan in the last 12 months. Some statistics indicate that 50% of the population do not have financial plans. If you haven't updated your plan in the last while, and your life situation has changed, now might be a good time to recalibrate and update your plan. Once you make updating your plan an annual habit, you will worry less about your future and no doubt will increase your financial security.

There are many organizations offering financial planning: financial institutions, credit unions, independent advisors, and more. Be very selective about the organization and individual you engage with. Note that some planners charge a fee, while others do not. They are commission based salespeople who make money from the mutual fund or GIC they sell you. On the other hand, independents typically offer financial planning for a fee and you can then select your investments.

Choosing the Right Advisor or Financial Planner

If you want to take the weight of the world off your shoulders, I suggest you get the help of a financial planner to help you achieve your financial goals. Most of them are experts and can therefore advise you on the appropriate strategy for your life stage and goals. However, planners and advisors are not created equal. Many are unfamiliar with the specific needs of women, how we think, and some of the particular challenges we face. According to the research of some psychology experts, advisors need a better understanding of the way women think. Many of us would agree that most financial institutions have not done a great job in creating women-friendly practices. This is evident through language, marketing strategies, and management styles. As stated by Kathleen Burns Kingsbury in her piece on "How to Give Financial Advice to Couples":

"The financial services industry prefers to treat all clients as gender neutral, even though there is clear evidence this is a mistake. Due to factors from how women are raised to how the female brain is wired, women communicate, relate and learn differently to men. Advisers need to appreciate these gender differences and tailor their approach in order to form trusting relationships with women. Finding the right advisor or planner that "fits" you is one of the most important things you will do for yourself. A good financial planning relationship can lead to successful financial outcomes for you."

We have gone through a detailed exercise in the last chapter where you mapped out your goals. This document listing your goals is your road map for the future. Each and every financial planner you meet must understand this contextual piece. Financial institutions will not engage in this type of planning with you, so the upside is you are now fully prepared to engage in conversations about your future and map out your financial resources in order to get you where you want to go. Financial planners must keep track of your long-term goals and the balance that will allow you the ability to live comfortably day-to-day. The plan must be delivered in person with a written report. An email report with a follow-up telephone call is not good enough.

Exercise

Over the next few weeks, do two things:

1. If you don't have a financial plan, find a financial planner in your community and set up an appointment. Now that you know what to expect, the process will be a lot easier. If you have an immediate need for any of the other five financial professionals I listed, ask your friends and family for referrals. I guarantee you will find someone suitable. I would suggest you spend the time in particular to find a financial planner who you can work with.

2. Start to familiarize yourself with the concept of investing and investing terms. Spend some time on Personal Finance Friday researching some of the companies I suggested earlier in this chapter. Remember, you are trying to increase your financial literacy and knowledge. You may not want to become an expert in self directed investing, but you need to have a baseline knowledge of the fundamentals.

Questions to Ask a Financial Planner

The Financial Planning Standards Council in Ontario, Canada, a respected organization in North America, has developed a list of questions to ask prospective planners. I would suggest you take the list with you and record your answers on a sheet of paper. Interview three prospective financial planners and ask them the same questions, so you can compare your notes and find the most suitable candidate. These questions will help you interview your three financial planners and help you choose a competent, qualified professional with whom you feel comfortable and whose business style suits your financial needs.
Don't be afraid to ask other questions as well. Any professional will welcome them.

What are your qualifications?
Many people offering financial services call themselves financial planners. However, financial planning is a detailed, comprehensive process. It requires hands-on experience and a strong technical understanding of topics such as personal tax planning, insurance, investments, retirement planning, and estate planning. It requires understanding of how a recommendation in one area can affect the others.

Ask the planner what qualifications inform their financial advice. Ask what training they have successfully completed. Ask what steps they have taken to keep up with changes and developments in the financial planning field.

Ask whether they hold any professional credentials including the Certified Financial Planner credential, which is recognized internationally as the mark of the competent, ethical, professional financial planner.

What experience do you have?

An important consideration in choosing any professional is their level of experience. Ask how long the planner has been in practice, the number and types of firms with which they have been associated, and how their work experience relates to their current practice. Inquire about what experience the planner has in dealing with people in similar situations to yours and whether they have any specialized training. Choose a financial planner who has at least two years experience in counselling individuals on their financial needs.

What services do you offer?

The services a financial planner offers will vary and depend on their credentials, registration, areas of expertise, and the organization for which they work. Some planners offer financial planning advice on a range of topics, but do not sell financial products. Others may provide advice only in specific areas such as estate planning or taxation. Those who sell financial products, such as insurance, stocks, bonds, and mutual funds, or who give investment advice, must be registered with provincial regulatory authorities and may have specialized designations in these areas of expertise.

> *"I think that more of our kids are ruined by the behaviour of their parents than by the amount of the inheritance."*
> **Warren Buffet (1930-) CEO**

What is your approach to financial planning?

The types of services a financial planner will provide vary from organization to organization. Some planners prefer to develop detailed financial plans encompassing all of a client's financial goals. Others choose to work in specific areas as clarified in the question above. Ask whether the individual deals only with clients with specific net worth and income levels. Also ask whether the planner will help you implement the plan they develop or refer you to others who will do so.

Will you be the only person working with me?

It is quite common for a financial planner to work with others in their organization to develop and implement financial planning recommendations. You may want to meet everyone who will be working with you. They often work with other professionals as well, including ones you already use, such as your lawyer and accountant.

How will I pay for your services?

Your planner should disclose in writing how she or he will be paid for the services provided. When planners are paid through commissions, they are compensated if you purchase financial products to implement a financial planning recommendation. In some cases, the commission is paid by the suppliers of financial products, such as an insurance company. In other cases, you pay the commission, for example, if you buy shares of a publicly traded company. Commissions are usually on a percentage basis.

> *"I rewrite my will every five or six years..."*
> **Warren Buffett (1930-) CEO**

Will and Estate Planning

Consumer Reports conducted a survey in 2012 on money habits in North America. They found that 86% of respondents said they hadn't created or updated their will and other estate planning documents in the past five years. This is concerning. You may be wondering why wills matter. If you don't have one you probably don't think you need one, but you are mistaken and I will tell you why.

If you have assets, you need a will. If you have dependents, you need a will. Many single women think they don't need a will because they don't have children, but in reality they too have valuable assets that need to be protected such as jewellery, houses, and cars. You should also be aware that, depending on the jurisdiction where you live, after two years, your common-law spouse has rights to your possessions. This varies by province, state, and country, but don't be caught off guard not knowing the laws of where you live. You not only need a financial planner, but may also need an estate lawyer. Many women struggle with issues such as pre-nuptial agreements, wills, and powers of attorney. The reason we struggle is because we avoid that which make us uncomfortable, and we often have inner struggles between our head and heart. Our minds tell us to do one thing while our hearts tell us to do something else. This inner conflict is the plight of most women.

However, when it comes to your money and your life, I encourage you to lead with your head and your heart will follow.

When your financial security is at stake, being logical and pragmatic will serve you better than being emotional. You need to make an intelligent and informed decision. A documented will ensures you are protected legally and that your wishes are recorded. Remember that anyone can contest a will and therefore it is essential that you have your will prepared by a will or estate lawyer. When someone disagrees with the contents of a will, they can contest it and make a claim against it. You don't want there to be any surprises after you are gone.

Having a will and estate plan will ensure that you and your family are protected should something happen. However, having a will is no guarantee of a smooth transition of your belongings and assets when you die. If you have a simple family structure or are single, there is little likelihood that you will be contested; but there is no guarantee. A will can be challenged by anybody if there isn't adequate provision for the proper maintenance and support of a spouse or dependent. It may be challenged if there is a mistake in the will; if fraud is suspected; if the mental capacity of the deceased is in question; if the deceased's state of mind prior to death was questionable; and/or if something in the will is not clear.

I recommend you spend some time getting your thoughts in order with a will-writing kit, but make no mistake you need to protect yourself further by taking it to a will and estate lawyer. Do not risk your children's future by not preparing. Your conversation with a trained professional will save you time, money, and heartache. Let's face it, creating your will is one of the most difficult processes you will go through in your life, but you can do it. If something changes in your life, such as you get married, you need to update your will. Most people don't and that is where the trouble begins. Make sure you protect yourself in the way that you want. Most women are unaware of the parameters around wills and possible contests. Even if you create a will, there is no guarantee it won't be contested.

Money does strange things to people, especially in families. Blended families offer a different set of circumstances and these need to be managed. Many single women believe they don't need to have a will, because they don't have a partner or children. They often see themselves as being different from their friends who have families and children. If you have assets you need a will. Many single women will bequeath their assets to nieces, nephews, siblings, and charities. Make your wishes known.

Money Story: Samantha

Samantha (Sam) comes from a very affluent blended family. Her mother married Joe, a man who was divorced with children from his previous relationship. Sam's stepfather, Joe, became the only father she ever knew. Joe's children from his previous relationship had grown up spoiled and wanting for nothing. They grew up with self-entitlement, believing their father's wealth should become their wealth. Sam's stepfather has embraced his new family whole heartedly; they have become the centre of his universe. He is a father, mentor, and friend to Sam. Joe has created what he believes to be an ironclad will. All his personal belongings, possessions, and wealth will pass to Sam's mother and his new family. Joe has chosen to leave nothing to the children from his first marriage; they are aware of his decision and it has created a permanent rift in the family. The family has now been split apart because of money. Joe's children will contest the will upon his death. Sam knows this and has already hired a lawyer to help her manage this eventuality.

Connecting with You

At this point, we are coming to the end of our journey of self-discovery and increasing your financial security. Our next chapter will highlight some global research and societal trends. Now might be a good time to talk about how you are feeling in this process so far. I hope your money energy has increased and that this journey is working for you in the way you wanted and even exceeding your expectations. You may be testing out some new language and new ways of looking at money. You are probably feeling yourself transforming. You have accomplished a lot in a very short period of time. Relying on others for your security can create economic helplessness. In contrast, strong relationships with everyone around you is empowering. Ask yourself the following questions:

1. Are you in a partner relationship with someone where the balance of power is off? If so, how do you plan to address this?

_____

_____

_____

_____

2. Have you created a will for yourself? If not, what is stopping you from getting one? If you have a will, have you updated it recently? If you haven't, now might be a good time to update it.

_____

_____

_____

_____

3. How do you feel about taking your Big Picture goals to meet with a financial planner or advisor?

_____

_____

_____

_____

4. How do you feel about finding a financial planner? Do you have any doubts holding you back?

_____

_____

_____

_____

Chapter Seven ~ The Perfect Storm for Women and Our Money

"We never know how high we are till we are called to rise; And then, if we are true to plan, our statures touch the sky."
Emily Dickinson (1830-1886) Poet

This chapter presents the socio-economic facts and insights about women and their money that are important for you to know as guiding lights into the world of self-discovery. Remember, being informed is one of our strategies. It is more important to think about what to do with the information presented to you, than the information itself. The challenges I am about to discuss demonstrate the importance of embracing the 6 Savvy Money Gal Strategies. I believe that being informed about the realities that confront us empowers us to action.

Women and the Glass Ceiling

The glass ceiling persists for many women. Some women earn up to 30% less than men performing the same job. 50% of marriages end in divorce. More and more single women have no shoulder to lean on. While some women have become major breadwinners in their families, others struggle to make ends meet. These facts are a call to action. What we do with our money matters, and it is vital to grow and protect our wealth in order to live comfortably into retirement.

Let's fully understand the obstacles that stand in the way. We may be making choices that unconsciously create our own glass ceiling! We have learned the importance of breaking patterns and the importance of standing in our own strength. We do this by embracing a winning mindset and looking to the future; living an authentic life within our means. We engage in mindful and conscious choices with our money and live by simple truths.

Our complicated financial world has created a perfect storm for women. We are living longer, and confront new concerns around aging, spending, and our health. Taking control of how you think and the choices you make are the cornerstones for you to weather the storm and attain financial success.

As women we are capable of doing anything, but we are often at a disadvantage economically, which keeps us from getting more from our lives and money. Recognize when you are facing a glass ceiling. If you cannot afford a purchase, you have reached a glass ceiling with your money. If your male colleague makes more than you at the same job, you are experiencing a glass ceiling.

> *"We can't solve problems by using the same kind of thinking we used when we created them."*
> **Albert Einstein (1879-1955) Theoretical Physicist**

Pushing through the glass ceiling requires a mentor to help you to understand company politics, and unwritten rules or protocol. One of my biggest obstacles to overcome was finding a mentor or champion. While working in corporate, I struggled to find someone. Most companies don't have formal mentoring programs. Therefore unless you are on a high potential list, you are doomed to find your own way to the top without help. It is difficult to trail braze without mentoring. Women require the right mentoring to succeed in the corporate world. Some believe that women need to be more like men in order to succeed. I have found that this is not true and when you try to be like someone else, you lose yourself. I was also not prepared to put in long hours while raising my family. The unwritten rules or requirements to get ahead did not align with my values. Many women I know have left the corporate world in order to find balance and to work for organizations that value the family demands of their employees.

On the bright side, I eventually found the right mentors to champion me in my quest to live a more authentic life. They helped me trail braze a new path and find purpose. This highlights the importance of remaining persistent and hopeful. Each of us has a glass ceiling in our life; it is possible to break through it. Look for opportunities or create your own by smashing through road blocks on your journey to reaching your full potential.

The percentage of women who fill executive officer positions at Fortune 500 companies is much lower compared to men, and the gap is even wider between the percentage of female and male CEOs, with male CEOs far outnumbering female CEOs. The glass ceiling women face is pervasive. It comes from the workplace, our own limiting beliefs, and the cultural mythology about women. Our desire for economic security is at the heart of our existence and we have to embrace the notion that, not only can we push through our own glass ceilings - the barriers we create for ourselves, but we can do this in every aspect of our lives. Circumstances are improving for women; however, change will only come when, as we rise, we consciously lift those around us in order to apply more pressure in breaking down barriers.

Money Story: Warren Buffett

Warren Buffett is a mentor of mine, but I have never met him. I follow his advice, philosophy, and approach to life. I deeply respect him. Warren Buffet is very vocal about his views on women, money, and the glass ceiling women encounter. His attitudes and beliefs reflect the zeitgeist of our time- he sees women slowly beginning to smash the glass ceiling. He was quoted as saying: "For most of our history, women -- whatever their abilities -- have been relegated to the sidelines … in recent years we have begun to correct that problem. But an even greater enemy of change may well be the ingrained attitudes of those who simply can't imagine a world different from the one they've lived in."

The cultural mythology that holds women back does not reflect the spirit of our times. Boomers and the silent generation may still be living in a world that consciously or unconsciously has a bias toward women, though younger women and women from the next generation may have released the baggage from the past.

Women growing up in the forties and fifties were expected to chart a certain course and not trail blaze in areas that were typically the male domain. Warren Buffet witnessed, at an early age, the prejudice against women through the lens of how his sisters of equal intelligence and ambition were treated and expected to chart a different course from his. They faced limiting beliefs about what was possible for them. They were defined by society's expectations. Warren Buffet recollects that, because he was born a boy, his opportunities trumped those of his sisters. For them, "marrying well" defined their success, not what they did with their lives. Financial security for women could only be achieved through marrying up, resulting in full economic reliance and dependence on their husbands. Warren was quoted as saying "so my floor became my sisters' ceiling -- and nobody thought much about ripping up that pattern until a few decades ago. Now, thank heavens, the structural barriers for women are falling." There is no better example I could find that demonstrates the realities women faced and continue to face to this day. The glass ceiling of money has its roots in societal expectations.

Let me share with you a money story about Penny. Most of us can identify with it, because it is the classic immigrant story, revealing that economic success is possible for anyone.

Money Story: Penny

Penny moved to Canada from a poor European country in the 1950s. As an uneducated immigrant, she had not learned to read and write. She worked in a factory, and made a very modest income. Yet, with her careful and thrifty habits and goal setting, Penny put both her daughters through university, had a rainy day fund, and lived in a nice neighbourhood. Most people would think she was very successful. Although she relied heavily on the help of her mother to care for her children while she worked, she was guided by her desire to give her children a better life through a North American education. This classic immigrant story is a real life example of how women view money as a resource to help them provide for their families. Family trumps all. A mother will do anything for her children and sacrifice much to give them a better life.

A new wave of immigrants is arriving in North America. They hold many of the same values and goals as Penny. Fortunately, they arrive in a country that is developed and thriving, where finding prosperity and some degree of assimilation may be easy. North America has become more conscious of the plight of new immigrants, and there are many programs and resources available today to help them adapt to their new life. This is promising.

Social Realities and Inequities That Women Face Today

> *"Prejudices, it is well known, are most difficult to eradicate from the heart whose soil has never been loosened or fertilized by education; they grow there, firm as weeds among rocks."*
> **Charlotte Brontë (1816-1855) Novelist and Poet**

Hillary Clinton, one of the most powerful women in the world, has experienced the wrath of prejudice first-hand. While she ran for the US presidential nomination in 2008, she faced discriminatory slurs, comments, and gestures. During an interview, she was asked questions unrelated to politics. Although the focus of the interview was politically related, the interviewer could not resist a question about clothes.

- Interviewer: Okay. Which designers do you prefer?
- Hillary Clinton: What, designers of clothes?
- Interviewer: Yes.
- Hillary Clinton: Would you ever ask a man that question?
- Interviewer: Probably not. Probably not.

The backdrop to this question is a society where women continually have to struggle for gender equality with men to prove their worth.

Many women thought the issue of equal pay for equal work would be resolved by now. One look at the gender make-up of corporate boards, clarifies how women continue to struggle to have their voices heard in a way that drives material change in our society. Society values assertiveness, self-confidence, and entrepreneurial skills, all of which tend to be ascribed as masculine attributes. Often when women reflect these attributes they are perceived as aggressive or abrasive. Research tells us that women are expected to be friendly, happy, and unselfish, and these attributes are programmed into our subconscious. Society can't arbitrarily tell women to be assertive, self-confident, and entrepreneurial when our subconscious has been taught otherwise.

If you question the research, conduct an experiment of your own and test this hypothesis. There is no doubt that these conflicting societal expectations hold women back. If we don't redefine how we think, we will never redefine how we act and what we do.

Society continues to tell women how to think, how to behave, and how to feel. We are told not to feel certain ways or to dismiss things that bother or ail us. All of us have heard, "it's just in your head." In our innate desire to be liked, get along with others, and create harmony, our minds and lives are cluttered with nonsense and mixed messages that hold us back from who we genuinely are and getting to where we want to go. The following story illustrates how inequitable reality can be for women.

Money Story: Kate

Kate grew up in a wealthy family in the city of Toronto. Money was never a concern until her father died suddenly. He passed unexpectedly, but not without leaving a comprehensive will. His will was clear and uncontested. Kate's brothers inherited the entirety of their father's money and nothing was left to Kate or her mother. The brothers vowed to share the very large estate with the family. That never happened. At a very young age, Kate learned the prejudice of being a girl and living in a patriarchal society. This experience shaped her views on money and her journey with money.

Today, she is not a bitter person. She is kind, generous, and spirited. Despite early trauma and adversity, she trained as a doctor and built a thriving practice. The prejudice and discrimination she faced as a young woman could have derailed her. It didn't. She learned to be brave, have courage and to stand in her own strength. I admire her deeply.

> *"I wanted him to cherish and approve of me, not as he had when I was a child, but as the woman I was, who had her own mind and made her own choices."*
> **Adrienne Rich (1929-) Poet, Theorist and Feminist**

Kate's example can inspire us all. A woman who is capable of standing in her own strength is empowered in a way that prepares her to define her future and create a life of prosperity and abundance.

> *"The great question that has never been answered, and which I have not yet been able to answer, despite my thirty years of research into the feminine soul, is 'what does a woman want?'"*
> **Sigmund Freud (1856-1939) Neurologist**

Connecting Emotional Well-Being and Life Evaluation

If money creates questions, you deserve to find the answers. Women know what they want in life. You know what you want because you have spent time creating your Big Picture goals and have defined a vision for yourself. As we recreate and redefine what is important, women are seeking love, happiness, health, and the peace of mind that comes with emotional well-being.

Recent research has begun to distinguish between two aspects of subjective well-being in which each feeds and strengthens the other, experts Daniel Kahneman and Angus Deaton identify these as emotional well-being and life evaluation. "Emotional well-being" refers to the emotional quality of an individual's everyday experience—the frequency and intensity of joy, stress, sadness, anger, and affection that makes one's life pleasant or unpleasant. "Life evaluation" refers to the thoughts that people have about their lives when they review past actions, events, and results. If you are feeling good about your situation and life you likely have an excellent dose of emotional well-being. If you don't feel good about your situation and you are stressed with worry, you probably could benefit from a boost to your emotional well-being.

The demands women face today are as great and complex as any generation that came before. In some aspects, the demands may be greater, as the pace of life is accelerating beyond belief. As mentioned earlier, money is a resource or tool that assists us in meeting our goals. Many women believe that if they had more money, all of their problems would be solved. For some, this is absolutely true. Managing money is never black and white, and women tend to have an emotional, financial, and spiritual connection with their money that makes managing it very complex.

Surveys show that 50% of women feel stressed about managing the household's money. Feeling overwhelmed about money reflects the pressure to make ends meet and to juggle the demands of family and work. The double-duty demands of home and workplace force many women to sacrifice their long-term economic security. This is a high price to pay for being a mother. Since women still shoulder most of the domestic load and still face wage discrimination, it's not surprising that – over their lifetime – they earn much less than men. We are working with less, therefore we need to be more vigilant to protect what we have.

The realities of everyday life have created the perfect storm for women and their money. It doesn't matter how much money you have or what generation you were born into, most of us want and hope for better outcomes with our money. Yet, no matter how much effort is expended, it remains challenging to get ahead. Incomes are not rising, they are not keeping up with the cost of living or inflation. It's like kissing one frog after the other and none of them ever turns into a prince. You continually see frog after frog staring you in the face.

For these very reasons, a healthy state of mind and positive emotional well-being are essential for coping with the demands of life and the stresses of managing your money. When a woman is strong and healthy, physically and emotionally, she is at peak-performance level; she sleeps well and is productive at work. If women are stressed by money concerns, there is little capacity to grow, solve their money problems, and take on more. Stress can lead toward depression, anxiety, and a whole series of emotional challenges that make coping with everyday life difficult. Women must prioritize their self-care, even in a busy schedule.

The Money Women Must Earn Creates Challenging Economic Realities

Women normally make less money than men. In order to achieve a good standard of living, we have to be more vigilant and consistent with our money management strategies. Women are living longer. The cost to fund our future healthcare needs, coupled with having less money, will challenge us in our older years.

Leaving the workforce to have and care for children may result in women earning less money in their careers, and possibly having a reduced pension when they retire. Women also often end up caring for their parents and managing their parents' money. Taking over the financial responsibility of an elderly parent can be daunting, and complex family dynamics often come into play.

On top of women living longer, often being paid significantly less than men, encountering financial problems due to divorce, and caring for elderly parents, women have the added responsibility of being our children's main teachers when it comes to managing money. Many schools do not teach about finance. It is often the mother who acts as the primary educator of children. Financially illiterate parents are unable to teach their children important financial lessons and the financial illiteracy cycle might continue to the next generation.

Personal Risks Women Face

Consider the diagram here that connects some of the most important personal risks that women face: the factors surrounding spending, divorce, healthcare, and longevity, which also carry the possible burden of outliving one's money.

The risk factors of spending, divorce, healthcare, and longevity are important themes. Not only do women contribute (either solely or in part) to their family's financial future, but we have entered into a time of unmatched concerns related to spending, health, and longevity. Longevity may mean living to the age of ninety or one hundred years old; no woman wants to run out of money. Let's dig a little deeper.

Longevity Comes with the Risk of Running Out of Money

In terms of longevity, women are living longer. At the age of forty, it's hard to imagine your life at sixty plus and so, because there are so many other financial priorities. Many of us don't start saving early enough for retirement. However, women are living well into their eighties and nineties; when you start saving early within even a small amount, the time value of money and compounding interest will get your money working for you when you retire. Retirement could be one of the longest, most relaxing and enjoyable phases in your life. Some leading experts have suggested that retirement could last a period of thirty to forty years. Recent Canadian research suggests that the average age of a widow is fifty six.

Spending

The spending that results in high consumer debt can erode wealth and limit savings. All of us must watch how we spend our money for this obvious reason. If women are living longer, we need more money to last a longer lifetime. If we spend it all when we are young, it won't be there for retirement. Finding the balance between enjoying life today and preparing for a long life is a juggling act for most women.

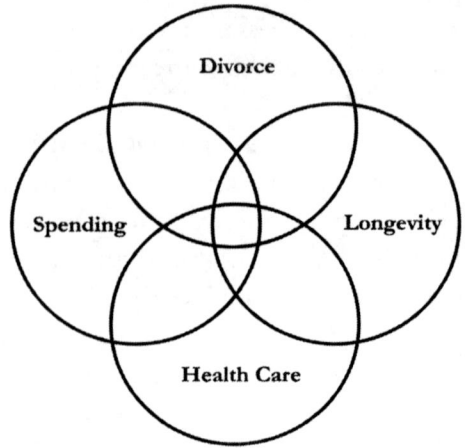

Divorce

Divorce creates another challenging economic reality for women. About one in five women fall into poverty as a result of divorce; about one in three who own homes have children living at home. When these women divorce, they and their children often lose the family home and end up in rental accommodation. Three out of four divorced mothers don't receive full or even partial payment of child support. Eight out of ten single parent families are headed by women, which adds up to one million households in Canada. This is alarming. Being poor increases the likelihood that a woman's children will also be poor. Women are likely to be single in retirement, due to high divorce rates and their tendency to outlive men. The average age of divorce is 56.

Women who leave a partner to raise children on their own are five times more likely to live in poverty than if they had stayed. Many of us know women who are single mothers living in poverty. It is heartbreaking. I openly admit that I would find it very difficult to give up my personal luxuries, comforts, and trappings.

Money Story: Mary

I worked with a young woman many years ago who was well educated with a Master's degree. She had a terrific job and was paid well. However, she found herself in an extremely verbally abusive marriage. I asked her why she stayed in the relationship and didn't leave. She told me that there would be economic consequences if she left her husband. The problem was not that she had simply grown accustomed to a comfortable lifestyle. The situation was complicated she told me, and because I was unmarried, she did not believe it was possible for me to understand. She was a devoted Catholic and believed very strongly in her vows of "to death us do part." Her strong religious vocation created pressures in her decision making process.

However, my view was that I did understand her situation. From my vantage point, I found it far too painful to witness her crying every day; while struggling with issues of self-esteem and self-worth. Also, I found it difficult to go along with her pretending the rest of the time that everything was okay. Nothing was okay. I have always wondered how life has treated her since we lost touch, and I sure hope that she has found a way to honour herself and gain self-esteem. Women sometimes stay in abusive relationships because leaving will plunge thems and their children into poverty.

The impacts of divorce on women are alarming, and many women who divorce may need to increase their income between 20% and 30% to maintain a decent standard of living; one in five could end up in poverty. If you are in a difficult marriage or are separated, you may want to think through the implications of divorce to your standard of living. Is there an opportunity to reconcile? Sometimes breaking the marriage bond is irreparable and no reconciliation is possible. I am not suggesting staying in an abusive relationship; what I am saying is that in situations where there has not been any abuse, sometimes it is too easy to walk away.

Money Story: Veronica

One woman I know who was childless, walked away from her family home and partner, and never turned back. She left a sizeable nest egg behind in not fighting for her family home, but her need to get away from her former husband was so strong, it trumped any desire or thought about her future financial security. And, although I don't recommend this drastic course of action, I understand why she did what she did. Some women will fight for years to get what they deserve financially, while others don't want to spend their lives fighting.

Healthcare

Finance expert Moshe Milevsky indicates that women need on average 21% more money in retirement than men need; much of this will be needed for healthcare expenses not covered by typical government pensions. Although this is retirement related, it reminds me, and must remind you, of the importance of caring for yourself now. Women have entered into a period of concerns around health that we have never seen before. We need to be more mindful of the importance of our health. When a health scare occurs everything in life changes. Having a cushion, an emergency fund, or a nest egg to fall back on can often be the answer to getting through life's health challenges.

Canadian Women's Foundation Mandate

The Canadian Women's Foundation (www.canadianwomen.org) has gathered and shared insightful research and information on the importance of helping women move themselves out of poverty. The data demonstrates that helping women break the cycle of poverty benefits not just themselves, but their children and their community.

Helping Low Income Women Strengthens their Children

When children live in poverty, it is usually because their mother lives on a low income. 80% of all single-parent families - over one million families - are headed by women. They are among the poorest in the country. The Canadian Women's Foundation's Fact Sheet- Moving Women out of Poverty highlights interesting statistics relating to women and poverty. According to Women in Canada- A Gender-Based Statistical Report – Economic Well-Being, single moms in Canada have a net worth of around $17,000, while single dads average a net worth around $80,000 (Net worth is the total value of the larger possessions, such as cars, furniture, real estate, savings, stocks, RRSPs, etc.)

Other research shows that for women living on low incomes, there may also be evidence of lower levels of emotional well-being, happiness, and life satisfaction. Women often sacrifice their own well-being to ensure the future of their children.

Why Women are More Likely to Live in Poverty

According to the Canadian Women's Foundation, women are more likely than men to live in poverty, for two main reasons:

- Each day, men and women work about the same number of hours, but women do more unpaid work (housework, childcare, meal preparation, eldercare, etc.) , leaving less time for paid work. Women spend an average of about 4.2 hours a day doing unpaid work, while men spend about 2.2 hours. (Derek Abma, Vancouver Sun, "Women carry the load of unpaid work in rich nations")
- Stay-at-home dads do less childcare (under 1.6 hours per day) than stay-at-home moms (3.1 hours per day).(Veerle Miranda, Cooking, Caring and Volunteering: Unpaid Work Around the World)

Women Juggling Demands of Paid and Unpaid Work

Women spend a lot of their time on cleaning the home, organizing, cooking meals, and taking care of their families. Unpaid work drains women of the energy needed for self-care, because it is often performed on top of full-time work in the labour force. Many women are pushed to work up to five (occasionally more) full days per week, as well as juggling the unpaid work demands of their home and family responsibilities. Unpaid work may go unacknowledged by many in a women's circle of friends and relatives, not to mention by a spouse or partner. With demanding schedules, women have relatively little spare time for themselves. This is the reality.

No amount of well-intentioned financial education will reach women when they have relatively little spare time to devote to learning. That is why when you manage your personal calendar with precision you control how you spend your time. Personal Finance Friday is a prescriptive and deliberate way for you to get a better handle on your money and to keep this time sacred for learning and increasing your knowledge. There is a false perception by many that literacy is the key to greater financial success for women performing unpaid work. I beg to differ. Finding better work-home life balance, and providing simple solutions in ways that resonate for women overburdened with the demands of paid and unpaid work, makes more sense.

Love and Unpaid Work: The Balancing Act

> *"In family life, love is the oil that eases friction, the cement that binds closer together, and the music that brings harmony."*
> **Eva Burrows (1929–)**
> **Australian Community Welfare Organizer**

The bottom line reason why women participate in so much unpaid work may be due to their proclivity toward expressing their love for other human beings. This dedication toward others may be the driving force behind why women often push themselves past the breaking point and past their own ability to remain emotionally, physically, spiritually, and mentally healthy.

> *"Money speaks sense in a language all nations understand."*
> **Aphra Behn (1640- 1689) Dramatist and Writer**

Women's lower earning power means they are at a higher risk of falling into poverty if they have children and then become separated, divorced, or widowed. They are less able to save for their retirement and more likely to live in poverty in their senior years. And, as previously mentioned, the fear of falling into poverty means that some women stay in abusive relationships, despite the dangers. Many women today pursue demanding careers and are very successful. However, the top female CEOs usually have partners who take on the bulk of the domestic work and childcare. When women work outside the home and also do most of the domestic work, their long-term health suffers. According to Statistics Canada, women at every age are more likely than men to describe their days as "quite a bit" or "extremely" stressful.

There is no disputing the facts unearthed in this current research. Many women might recognize themselves somewhere in the facts and figures, as well as in the underlying themes. Although this research is Canadian-based, I would like women reading this from other parts of the world to think about the plight of women who live in poverty in their country. "Women in poverty" is a global issue, and the more each of us become aware of the real facts, we can better engage in driving social and material change in ways that would benefit our own communities. Remember, it takes a village to raise a child and a global movement to raise women out of poverty.

The intent here is to inform you of the economic realities women face. This is the context. And, one of the main themes to focus on is that the impact of living in poverty can and does have huge implications on a woman's emotional well-being, quality of life, and her happiness. Living in the reality or consciousness of poverty is a significant roadblock that challenges many women's abilities to stand in their own strength. In addition, remaining in any kind of toxic relationship or partnership for economic comfort will also result in a woman who is unable to live authentically and stand in her own strength.

In most instances, higher education means higher income. Therefore, it is important to prepare for the future by going back to school to pursue a college certificate or diploma and, if feasible, an undergraduate, master's or doctorate degree. It is important for women to continually think about upgrading their education, so that they can make up for money lost during the childbearing and stay-at-home years.

The Silver Lining for Some Women

Even though hard economic realities exist for women, there are some silver linings; positive economic news for women is available and there appears to be increasing incidents of good news arising all the time.

Women could find themselves suddenly rich because of what is being termed as the "baby boomer wealth transfer." A leading American bank, State Street, released statistics in May 2013 that indicated that women own 51.3% of wealth in the US, or assets valued at more than eight trillion dollars. They believe it will increase to twenty-two trillion dollars by 2020. Over the next forty years, women are expected to inherit 70% of the forty-one trillion dollars in inter-generational wealth transfers. Increasing your financial capability matters more than ever!

Also, an encouraging number of global icons are advocating about the positive impact women have and are making on society. In a recent interview, Warren Buffet noted that we have reached a cross-road in which women's issues must be everyone's issues. Society can only benefit by this.

This chapter covers a great deal of ground. Money pressures are real for women and the backdrop of the economic realities today create a harsh environment for many of us. Managing our money better and finding more financial security has never been more relevant. Making your money a priority is the way to plant the seeds of change for your future. Without major societal changes, the burden will continue to fall on women's shoulders, but each and every one of you can do something about this. Inevitably, it is better to be informed and learn to navigate through this, than to be an ostrich in the sand who takes the avoidance approach. Avoidance is easy and is often a common response we have when we don't like something or want it to go away. The self awareness you now have will help you navigate the realities of life.

Chapter Eight ~ Conclusion
Your Financial Security

Happiness + Energy + Power = Financial Security

The glass ceiling women face is pervasive, but it does not have to be that way, and I hope I have been able to demonstrate to you that with a winning mindset and greater consciousness you can make choices that result in better outcomes for yourself and greater financial security. When we allow limited self belief to permeate our minds, we create a mental block that holds us back. Managing the clutter and noise around you and being aware of popular culture's depiction of women is a must.

We have to embrace the notion that we as women can not only can push through the corporate glass ceiling, but we can do this in every aspect of our lives. We have discussed how the "glass ceiling" is a metaphor for the barriers that we create for ourselves, as well as those that others create for us. Circumstances are changing for women, and with champions such as Warren Buffet, Hillary Clinton and Michelle Obama speaking out for the empowerment of women, the plight of women will improve. Together our voices will help squash limiting beliefs about women, which keep us from reaching our full potential.

Women are becoming the major bread winners in many families. With this will come a new set of circumstances. Many women continue to struggle to make ends meet. Incomes are not growing and keeping up with the cost of living. We are living with less money every day; while the cost of living rises. The socio-economic backdrop for women has never been more diverse, challenging, and complex. The majority of women today work in the labour force and participate in the world economy. It is thus inevitable that money and power will define women in the same ways that men have traditionally been defined. For women, that definition must resonate with our values and belief systems.

Cultural forces and mythologies have taught women the importance of being "good girls", and that fitting in and being liked are expected. Women who challenge the status quo may find themselves feeling like outsiders, but they also usually recognize that conscious social change is more important than fitting in or being popular. For those women who find themselves increasingly, or even fully, enlightened and self-aware, an enormous amount of unwavering self-confidence is required. For these women it is impossible to follow the herd and be one of the sheep. It becomes mandatory to define a path that feels right.

Money worries and concerns can create undue hardship and pain for many of us. Expanding your mind will allow you to take control of your life and money. We have taken a journey to teach you to believe in yourself and manage your nagging doubts by embracing a winning mindset. We spent time helping you figure out that leaving your money pasts behind and living a clutter-free life is freeing. As you continue to learn to live your life more authentically, and make savvy choices, you are free to live your life with less worry, shame or embarrassment. Remember the past is the past.

Financial security and abundance are based upon self-awareness and cultivating emotional well-being through skill based learning that will transform your life. Taking a principle and value centred approach to your life and your money is essential. When we live by our values, we are guided by a more powerful force that naturally and easily encourages improvements in our lives.

Living a value centred life is the foundation to moving away from economic helplessness to economic empowerment. This matters for women because we are living longer and don't want to run out of money in our golden years. We have a new set of circumstances to manage around our spending, longevity, health, and navigating our lives. With this reality comes the need to redefine and re-evaluate everything we do. When your money and your future become priorities in your life, you will naturally and easily achieve successful outcomes.

Benefits of Living a Value-Centered Life

We have gone on a journey of self discovery to recreate ourselves and to redefine how we think about our lives and our money. We have engaged in some thought provoking exercises and have reviewed global trends. The strategies offered seek to help all of us find greater financial security and abundance in life. By embracing the Savvy Money Gal strategies you have made a conscious choice to live better and get more of what you need and want in life.

- You are actively engaging in mindful choice to manage your thoughts, emotions, energy, and surroundings.
- Your mind is clutter-free. You find more balance.
- You actively manage negativity that can erode your self-belief.
- You are far more aware of the cultural mythologies about women and money, and how they play out in society and at home. And each time you push at the glass ceiling of money and life, you help yourself and other women get one step closer to shattering the glass ceiling holding us all back.
- You know your life stage priorities and how to manage unexpected life events and life transitions.
- You understand that when your life is in motion, so is your money.

- You understand your money values and the impact they have had on your decision making.
- You have a clear vision for yourself and your future.
- You engage in conscious choice and have a clear understanding about whether you are a spendthrift or a tightwad. You understand the difference between short and long term thinking, and are finding more joy in saving money.
- You have a spending plan that keeps you focused on what matters. You no longer squander your money on things that really don't make you happy. You indulge in life's simple luxuries, because you know they matter and will help you find more joy and meaning in your life.
- You are actively engaged in building your personal wealth by investing more.
- You have a financial plan and you know who to turn to should an unexpected life event occur or if you want to plan ahead.
- You are no longer alone on your journey to finding financial security.

Many of us have thought that if we had more money we would be happier. We now know this is not true. It is how we manage and spend our money that can make the difference between a good and a great life. This is all within our control and power. Being more conscious and aware of the choices we make is a recipe for happiness. More money does not guarantee more happiness.

The facts speak for themselves. Women are living longer. A healthy sixty-five year old couple has a one in two chance of living to the age of ninety-two. And most likely it will be the woman who outlives the man. Many of the lifestyle choices women make will directly impact our economic well-being in the future. Once we move towards positive thinking, and manage the stereotypes and cultural mythology around women and money, we will find more inner peace and calm. We will worry less and focus more on living.

Our emotional well-being is linked to our physical and emotional health. Wealthy people do have longer lives, better nutrition, less anxiety, more time for friends and family — all things that contribute to contentment — yet their reported level of happiness is surprisingly not that much greater than people who have less. Health is the best form of wealth we can have. Taking care of ourselves by finding balance creates peace of mind. Being more positive creates a psychological boost and increases our emotional well-being.

Along our journey together, we have laughed and cried. We have left behind our past money mistakes. What trigged us in the past no longer triggers us today. We are more mindful and conscious of our thoughts and actions. We had moments of doubt and questioned the process. Our lack of belief was mostly stirred by our lack of self-belief, which no longer exists. We learned that when we make our money a priority, we can transform any bad habit and start fresh on a journey towards greater financial security.

When we live a value based life, we find financial security because we stand in our own strength, live authentically, make conscious choices, look to the future, and embrace a winning mindset. We are directing our money in ways that set us free and smashing the glass ceiling of money that holds many women back. Every woman on this earth has a money glass ceiling; once we make intelligent and savvy choices, we will no longer be held back by the shackles of the past or by cultural mythology.

Money is a powerful tool in our lives because we now know how to harness its power. Economic helplessness is no longer an option for women. We no longer accept money bullies in our lives, people who seek to dominate and control us to fuel their insecurities. A woman can stand in her own strength.

Find laughter for your money soul. Try not to take life too seriously. Find humour in small things, without mocking people. Enjoy simple pleasures, luxuries and joys. Don't forget to smile, because smiling for thirty seconds will reboot your entire system and make you feel good. Don't forget to hug your huggable friends and loved ones.

Evaluate how you live your life each and every day and be mindful of the choices you are making. When you are on-purpose, meaning you are living an authentic life, you will continue to put pressure on any economic glass ceiling you face. When you see dysfunctional behaviour around you, and trust me you will, you will not be negatively impacted, rather you will point the person in the right direction. As you become a role model, don't forget to lift up those around you. Show the way to financial security to those you care about, but don't promote their economic helplessness.

A Savvy Money Gal always keeps a healthy level of scepticism. Don't believe everything anyone tells you, but do not become mistrustful of everyone and everything either. Seek to understand and get the facts.

Keep the 6 Savvy Money Gal Strategies With You at All Times

Savvy Money Gal Strategy #1: Adopt a Winning Mindset around Money
Savvy Money Gal Strategy #2: Stop Living in the Past and Look to the Future
Savvy Money Gal Strategy #3: Be Authentic: Don't Live Beyond Your Means
Savvy Money Gal Strategy #4: Be Conscious of Your Life and Money Choices
Savvy Money Gal Strategy #5: Organize Your Life and Money
Savvy Money Gal Strategy #6: Rely on Yourself for Your Financial Security

While you focus on yourself and not others, your self-belief will continue to soar. Whenever you are in doubt about your money, you know who to turn to for expert advice. You are no longer alone on your journey to financial success. Money health is the best form of wealth, and by standing in your own strength you will break through any glass ceiling life or money presents.

And finally, if you marry, marry for love because you are a Savvy Money Gal who can make her own money and stand in her own strength!

I encourage you to evaluate how you live daily and to make informed and conscious choices. Don't say yes, when you mean no. Be ever present in your life when you make decisions and ground them in facts. Learn to enjoy and be grateful for what you have today. The money will come if you are on-purpose and doing what you love, want, and need.

Each and every day, I want you to ask yourself three very simple questions:

- Am I on purpose?
- Am I creating a life of meaning and joy?
- Am I ever present and conscious of the choices I make?

If you follow this simple formula and ask yourself these questions every day, you will continue to push yourself forward. Your emotional well-being will sky-rocket and you will worry less about money, be less fearful of your future, and manage any self-doubt that comes your way.

Stay focused on your goals. Let me know how you are doing by reaching out to me at info@ savvymoneygal.com. I want to hear from you – the good, the bad, and the ugly.

All my Best,
Anita

P.S. Keep saying your daily personal affirmation. Keep evolving it as you grow. Your personal affirmation at the start might not be your personal affirmation now. Look at how much you have grown.

P.P.S. Honor your investment by continuing to invest in yourself. Continue to make your money a priority and be a role model for others. You will feel great.

P.P.P.S. Love who you are becoming.

Bibliography

Abma, Derek. "Women carry the load of unpaid work in rich nations." Vancouver Sun, March 5 2011.

Allen, Colin. "The Benefits of Meditation." Psychology Today. Last modified June 6, 2012. http://www.psychologytoday.com/articles/200304/the-benefits-meditation

American Savings Education Council. Employee Benefit Research Institute. Accessed March 2013. http://www.ebri.org/education/

Anthony, Mitch. Life Transitions Top Ten Report. Mitch Anthony's Institute for Financial Life Planning, 2007.

"BMO Psychology of Spending Report: Impulse Shopping a Costly Habit for Canadians." Marketwire. Last modified September 25, 2012. http://newsroom.bmo.com/press-releases/bmo-psychology-of-spending-report-impulse-shoppin-tsx-bmo-201209250821167001

Buffett, Warren. The Snowball: Warren Buffett and the Business of Life. New York: Bantam, 2008.

Buffett, Warren. "Warren Buffett is bullish … on women." CNN Money. Last modified May 2, 2013. Accessed June 2013. http://money.cnn.com/2013/05/02/leadership/warren-buffett-women.pr.fortune/index.html

Burns Kingsbury, Kathleen. "How to Give Financial Advice to Couples." KBK Wealth Connection: Creating wealth from the inside out. Last modified 2013. http://www.kbkwealthconnection.com

Chu, Linda. Out of Chaos: Professional Organizing Solutions. Personal Interview August 2013. http://www.outofchaos.ca/

Clements, Jonathan. "Putting a Price Tag on Life's Financial Goals." Citi Bank Citi Blog. December 17, 2012. http://blog.citigroup.com/2012/12/putting-a-price-tag-on-lifes-financial-goals.shtml

Comuzzi, Dr. Catherine. Direct quotes from Dr. Catherine Comuzzi 2013. http://ccomuzzi. com

ConsumerReports.org. Accessed January 2013. http://www.consumerreports.org/

Covey, Steven R. The 7 Habits of Highly Effective People. New York: Free Press, 1989.
Cox, Kathleen. "We all want to be housewives now." The Age: Life & Style. Last modified January 10, 2011. Accessed April 2013. http://www.theage.com.au/lifestyle/life/we-all-want-to-be-housewives-now-20110110-19ka0.html

Deaton, Kahneman, Farrer, Straus, and Giroux. "High income improves evaluation of life but not emotional well-being." Psychological and Cognitive Sciences 107, no. 38 (2010): 16489-16493.

Dunn, Elizabeth and Norton, Michael. Happy Money: The Science of Smarter Spending. New York: Simon &
Schuster, 2013.

Duxbury, Linda and Higgins, Christopher. "Carleton Releases 2012 National Study on Balancing Work and Caregiving in Canada." Carleton Newsroom. Last modified October 25, 2012. Accessed March 2013. http://newsroom.carleton.ca/2012/10/25/carleton-releases-2012-national-study-on-balancing-work-and-caregiving-in-canada-linda-duxbury-to-talk-about-findings-at-building-healthier-workplaces-conference/

Erickson, Beth. Quoted in Satran, Richard. "5 Ways Sharing Finances Can be Bad for Your Marriage." US News and World Report. http://money.usnews.com/money/personal-finance/mutual-funds/articles/2013/05/07/5-ways-sharing-finances-can-be-bad-for-your-marriage

"Fact Sheet: Moving Women Out of Poverty." Canadian Women's Foundation. http://www.canadianwomen.org/sites/canadianwomen.org/files/

Financial Planning Standards Council: http://www.fpsc.ca/10-questions-ask-your-planner

FINRA Investor Education Foundation. "Take the Financial Literacy Quiz." National Financial Capability Study. Last modified 2013. http://www.usfinancialcapability.org/quiz.php

Freedman, David H. "Time-Warping Temptations." Scientific American Mind 24, no. 1 (2013): 45-49.

Gallup-Healthways. Well-Being Index. http://www.well-beingindex.com
"Get More Out of Life." Certified Financial Planner: Financial Planning Standards Council. Last modified January 2011. http://www.fpsc.ca/sites/fpsc.ca/files/documents/Get_more_out_of_life.pdf

Huffington Post. "Hillary Clinton On What Designers She Wears: 'Would You Ever Ask A Man That Question?'" HuffPost Style. Last modified May 25, 2011. http://www.huffingtonpost.com/2010/12/02/

Intuit: Simplify the business of life. Accessed May 2013. http://www.intuit.com

Maslow, Abraham. Motivation and Personality. New York: Harper & Row, 1954.

McKenna, Barrie. "Debt by numbers- Troubling trends in Canadian consumer spending." The Globe and Mail, August 28 2013.

"Media Release: Australian pocket money economy sits at $1.4 billion per annum." Commonwealth Bank of Australia. Last modified February 4, 2013. Accessed February 2013. https://www.commbank.com.au/about-us/news/media-releases/2013/australian-pocket-money-economy-sits-at-1-4-billion-pa.html

Merrill Lynch 2013 Survey in Satran, Richard. "5 Ways Sharing Finances Can be Bad for Your Marriage." US News and World Report. http://money.usnews.com/money/personal-finance/mutual-funds/articles/2013/05/07/5-ways-sharing-finances-can-be-bad-for-your-marriage

Milevsky, Moshe A. and Macqueen, Alexandra. Pensionize Your Nest Egg: How to Use Product Allocation to Create a Guaranteed Income for Life. Mississauga, Wiley & Sons Canada, Ltd: 2010.

Miranda, Veerle. "Cooking, Caring and Volunteering." Organisation for Economic Co-operation and Development. March 2011. http://www.oecd-ilibrary.org/social-issues-migration-health/

Rattiner, Susan. Women's Wit and Wisdom: A Book of Quotations. USA: Dover Publications, 2000.

Scott, Rick, Cryder, Cynthia, and Loewenstein, George. "Tightwads and Spendthrifts." Journal of Consumer Research 34, no. 6 (2008): 767-782.

Silva, Mark. "Michelle Obama: '120-percenter' Blog." Chicago Tribune: Mayflower Voyage. Last modified May 7, 2009. http://www.chicagotribune.com/topic/arts-culture/history/colonists-of-north-america/

Silverstein, Michael J. and Sayre, Kate. Women Want More. New York: HarperCollins, 2009.

Soman, Dilip and Mazar, Nina. "Financial literacy is not enough." The Hill Times 24, no 1165 (2012): 25. http://www.hilltimes.com/opinion-piece/politics/2012/11/26/financial-literacy-is-not-enough/32950

State Street Bank Source. SPDR University. Last modified 2013. http://www.spdru.com/

Stevenson, Betsey and Wolfers, Justin. "Subjective Well-Being and Income: Is There Any Evidence of Satiation?" American Economic Review. Last modified April 16, 2013. http://www.brookings.edu/~/media/research/files/papers/2013/04/

Tuttle, Brad. "A Mom's Work is Worth $113K Annually. Or Maybe About Half That." Time: Business & Money. Last modified April 30, 2012. Accessed March 2013. http://business.time.com/2012/04/30/a-moms-work-is-worth-113k-annually-or-maybe-about-half-that/

US Department of Labour. "Good for Business: Making Full Use of the Nation's Human Capital – The Environmental Scan – A Fact-finding Report of the Federal Glass Ceiling Commission." March 1995. http://www.dol.gov/dol/aboutdol/history/reich/reports/ceiling.pdf

"VIP Forum." CEB Wealth Management Leadership Council. Accessed March 2013. https://vip.executiveboard.com/Public/Default.aspx

Weekes, Karen. Women Know Everything! 3,241 Quips, Quotes & Brilliant Remarks. Philadelphia: Quirk Books, 2007.

Williams, Cara. "Women in Canada: A Gender-based Statistical Report- Economic Well-Being." Statistics Canada. December 2010. http://www.statcan.gc.ca/pub/89-503-x/2010001/article/11388-eng.pdf

Investing Terms

Stock exchanges: A stock exchange is a place where buyers and sellers meet to exchange-purchase and sell- stocks, bonds, and other investments. In its simplest form, it is a meeting place. The New York Stock Exchange is the largest in the world, based on market capitalization and the number of trades conducted. In the old days, people would meet in person to buy and sell shares of a company. Today, most trades are done electronically. Major stock exchanges in North America include, The New York Stock Exchange, The TSX or Toronto Stock Exchange, and NASDAQ. Around the world, the major stock exchanges are the Tokyo Stock Exchange, London Stock Exchange, and Hong Kong Stock Exchange.

Asset allocation: This is a process whereby someone spreads their money across a broad range of asset classes in order to reduce risk. For example, you could have an asset allocation of 40% in stocks, 40% in bonds, and 20% in cash. Asset allocation is typically used to reduce risk and exposure to the market. For someone who is risk adverse, they may have more money in cash or bonds. For those who are higher risk tolerant, assets could be as high as 60% in stocks. Much of this depends on age, time to retirement, need for funds, and risk tolerance. If a person cannot afford to lose any money, their risk tolerance would be lower. Many women have lower risk tolerance than men. This is a proven fact and we need to be mindful of this in our conversations about investing.

Common shares: These shares are available for purchase on a stock exchange and represent a portion of a company that the company has sold off to investors. Many of you will have heard about common shares of major companies in North America.

Inflation: Inflation refers to the process through which the growing price of goods and services rises and falls over time. As prices rise, money purchases less. As prices fall (which is not often) money purchases more. Inflation impacts what is called "purchasing power", which is how much you can get with $1.00. Countries use a term called CPI- or the consumer price index- to measure changes over time. Inflation can erode your ability to afford things. If inflation is rising at 2% and someone is only earning 1% in their savings account, their money is not keeping up with inflation. And this example does not even factor in taxes. On the other hand, money invested in a common share that is growing and earning 8% per year with inflation at 2%, allows someone to be further ahead in their ability to purchase things.

Liquidity: This refers to how easily an investment can be turned into cash should it be needed. A money market fund, for example, can easily be turned into cash.

Mutual funds and exchange traded funds: Many new investors will invest money in mutual funds, otherwise known as exchange traded funds. They are simply a basket of stocks. They trade on the stock exchange, like stocks, and they can hold other investments, such as bonds and commodities.

Diversification: This is a term used to describe the process of spreading out investments over different investment categories. For example, someone could diversify their portfolio between different bonds and stocks, or between different industries - oil and gas, banking, forestry, mining, etc. The benefits to diversifying an investment is that it potentially reduces risk by creating a balance between highs and lows.

Risk tolerance: This term refers to the level of risk involved in investing. Most women I know have a low tolerance for risk, especially with our money. We guard it. We protect it. However, in order to engage in investing, we need to get more comfortable with the risks involved in the stocks and bonds market, as opposed to putting money into a savings account.

Time value of money: The phrase "money doubles every seven years" means that if someone has invested $1.00, in seven years it will be worth $7.00. This reveals that the longer money is invested, the more it is capable of growing.

Difference between stocks and bonds: A stock is a share of a company, a type of security that represents ownership and a claim on part of the company's earnings and assets. There are two main types of stock: common and preferred. A common stock usually entitles the owner to vote at shareholders' meetings and to receive dividends. Preferred stocks generally do not have voting rights, but have a higher claim on assets and earnings than common shares. Owners of preferred stocks receive dividends before common shareholders and have priority in the event that a company goes bankrupt and is liquidated.
A bond is considered a debt instrument. It is a certificate that a company or the government can issue, promising to pay the holder a specific amount of interest for a specific length of time, and to repay the loan on maturity. Assets are generally pledged as security for a bond issue. Bonds trade like stocks. They pay interest at set amounts on regular or specific dates. Companies will issue bonds and sell them to the public, because in some countries it is a cheaper way for a company to get financing than through common shares or stocks.

Dollar cost averaging: Dollar cost averaging (DCA) is an investment strategy in which someone invests in equal amounts of a stock on a regular basis over a period of time. For example, someone might invest $100 a month for five years to purchase shares of Rogers Communications. When they do this, the share value will change at different times, averaging the dollar cost of the shares.

Fees and commissions: It doesn't matter who we work with or what type of investments we buy, we will be charged fees. Make sure you ask what the fees are for any particular investment.

Bull market: This is when a group of stocks or securities are expected to rise. Often people will say they are bullish about a stock, meaning they expect it to rise. Or someone may say I am bullish about the market, which means they anticipate the market rising or the price of stocks rising.

Bear market: A bear market is opposite to a bull market. This is when a group of stocks or securities are expected to decline. Often people will say they are bearish about a stock, meaning they expect it to drop or fall. Or someone may say I am bearish about the market, which means they anticipate the entire market dropping or falling.

Creating Savvy Money Gal Circles

If you enjoyed reading this book and found value in the exercises and approach, you might want to consider sharing your wealth with others. I have no doubt that you know of other like-minded women who would love to engage in a financial security circle to support each other on the road to financial success. As you actively manage your money better and differently, you will encounter speed bumps that may appear to stand in your way. Nothing is more empowering than chatting with other women who may be facing similar challenges and working together to find solutions. I would suggest you reach out to your friends and contacts first. Here are some guidelines to get you started:

Contact like-minded women: Engaging women you know, and their friends, is a great way to encourage participation in your financial security group. Make sure you keep the number manageable. I would suggest no more than eight to ten women.

Group think: You will need to actively manage group think. This is when a bunch of people get to know each other so well and become so comfortable that you start to see things similarly. In order to have healthy conversations, you must engage in conversations that are diverse and open. Different opinions matter and if one person seems to be dominating the discussion, they need to share "in the sand box." A dominant voice should not skew others' thinking.

Set agendas: For the first few meetings, setting an agenda might be tough, but I would encourage you to get input from others in terms of what they want to discuss. You can start off by engaging in meetings around each of our 6 Savvy Money Gal Strategies. You can expand your topics to include things that are really relevant, timely, and in the news. Remember, the goal of these groups is to empower mindful change and greater self-awareness. You need to hold each member accountable to the other. Avoid a self-appointed leader. Give each member a chance to chair and run the meeting. This will build leadership skills for all the members. The more engaged women are, the more likely they will be to show up and participate.

Sharing your thoughts: There has to be an unwritten rule that what you share in the room stays in the room. It is kind of like the old Vegas saying: "what happens in Vegas, stays in Vegas." I would not encourage women to share all their financial statements unless they feel the group can help. You will have to create some of your own norms around how you want to run the sessions.

Have fun: The meetings must be fun. Bring chocolate or other goodies to lighten the mood. Talking about life and money can easily turn serious. Keep it light. Bring tissues, because talking about money comes with sharing a few tears. And also remember that anger is an emotion of growth. If your group gets angry from time to time, take the anger and turn it into action.

Learn to listen: One of the hardest things for all of us to do is listen. We want to jump to solutions first, but listening keeps us focused on what a person says. You must keep your eyes open and listen to the pain others are ready to share.

Take ownership: I would suggest you continue to take ownership for your own personal life and financial goals. Remember, try not to take on other people's problems, because this will not help anyone move away from economic helplessness. Helplessness is learned behaviour. You want to foster empowerment and growth.

Meeting frequency: Meet once every three weeks and hold people accountable for attending the meeting. Choose a new location each week to keep things fresh with a change of scenery. If you have a location that works and that everyone likes coming to, then don't change it. The goal is to encourage attendance and have fun. Managing money can be fun. Remember when you expand your mind, you can expand your savings and how you manage money.

Author Biography

Anita Saulite, MBA and Certified Life Coach, is the CEO of Savvy Money Gal (www.savvymoneygal.com). She is committed to strengthening women's financial security through skill-based learning. She provides a broad range of services to help women boost their emotional well-being around money and get on the path to financial success. For 20 years, she has worked at major financial institutions, including most recently as a Senior Manager at BMO Bank of Montreal. Anita has presented on several topics relating to women and personal finance, and is also a volunteer mentor with the Forum for Women Entrepreneurs. She has developed award winning educational and skill-based learning programs, and has been featured as a guest on The Pattie Lovett-Reid Show (CTV) and on Global BC1 News. Currently living in Vancouver with her husband and son, this Savvy Money Gal is also a hockey mom who enjoys swimming, gardening, and travel.

Anita Saulite, MBA is a developer of award winning skill-based learning programs in North America and a thought leader on women's issues. She shares her insight, deep knowledge, and savvy money strategies through keynote presentations, client workshops, loyalty driving programs, and personal one-on-one coaching. As a speaker, Anita shares inspiring and remarkable money stories of women who have redefined money in their lives. She seeks to raise women's consciousness around money for better choices and outcomes.

To learn more about Anita Saulite, visit her at:

Website
www.savvymoneygal.com

Facebook
www.facebook.com/SavvyMoneyGal

LinkedIn
www.linkedin.com/in/anitasaulite

Twitter
www.twitter.com/savvymoneygal

CPSIA information can be obtained at www.ICGtesting.com
Printed in the USA
LVOW11s1503220114

370536LV00009B/605/P